THE KEYNES SOLUTION

THE KEYNES SOLUTION

The Path to Global Economic Prosperity

PAUL DAVIDSON

THE KEYNES SOLUTION
Copyright © Paul Davidson, 2009.

First published in 2009 by PALGRAVE MACMILLAN® in
the United States—a division of St. Martin's Press LLC,
175 Fifth Avenue, New York, NY 10010.

Where this book is distributed in the UK, Europe, and the rest of
the world, this is by Palgrave Macmillan, a division of Macmillan
Publishers Limited, registered in England, company number 785998,
of Houndmills, Basingstoke, Hampshire RG21 6XS.

Palgrave Macmillan is the global academic imprint of the above
companies and has companies and representatives throughout
the world.

Palgrave® and Macmillan® are registered trademarks in the United
States, the United Kingdom, Europe, and other countries.

ISBN: 978–0–230–61920–3

Library of Congress Cataloging-in-Publication Data

Davidson, Paul, 1930–
    The Keynes solution / by Paul Davidson.
        p. cm.
    Includes bibliographical references and index.
    ISBN 978–0–230–61920–3
        1. Keynesian economics. 2. Keynes, John Maynard, 1883–1946.
    I. Title.

HB99.7.D392 2009
330.15′6—dc22   2009009558

A catalogue record of the book is available from the British Library.

Design by Newgen Imaging Systems, Ltd., Chennai, India

First edition: September 2009

10 9 8 7 6 5 4 3 2 1

Printed in the United States of America.

To my wonderful, always supportive family—
Louise, Robert, Fanny, Christopher, Emily, Kai,
Diane, Dan, Greg, Tamah, Arik, Gavi, and Zakkai

CONTENTS

ACKNOWLEDGMENTS

I could not have written this book without the help and understanding that my wife, Louise, always gives to all my endeavors.

I also wish to thank Laurie Harting, my editor at Palgrave Macmillan, for the immense help, advice, and encouragement she provided as I wrote these chapters.

Chapter 1

THE POWER OF IDEAS TO AFFECT POLICY

[T]he ideas of economists and political philosophers, both when they are right and when they are wrong, are more powerful than is commonly understood. Indeed the world is ruled by little else.

—John Maynard Keynes

Politicians and talking heads on television are continuously warning the public that the current economic crisis that began in 2007 as a small subprime mortgage default problem in the United States has created the greatest economic catastrophe since the Great Depression of the 1930s. What is rarely noted, however, is that what is significant about this current global economic and financial crisis is that its origin lies in the operations of free (unregulated) financial markets. Yet for more than three decades, mainstream academic economists, policymakers in government, and central bankers and their economic advisors have insisted that: (1) both government regulations of markets and large government spending policies are the cause of our economic problems, and (2) ending big government and freeing markets from government regulatory controls is the solution to our economic problems.

By the autumn of 2008, it became clear that the liberalized financial markets of the twenty-first century could not heal the bloodletting catastrophe that they had caused. In October 2008, the United States Secretary of the Treasury and former head of a major investment bank, Henry Paulson, went to Congress to request an unprecedented $700 billion in funds to bail out private financial institutions that, in earlier years, had made spectacular profits from their operations in these liberalized financial markets. The chief officers of these financial service institutions had been rewarded in salaries and bonus sums that only a decade earlier would have seemed equivalent to the income of a king in a fairy tale.

As the situation worsened every day during that autumn, it soon became clear that this financial bailout would not be sufficient to restore a prosperous economy. Governments around the world began to recognize the need for a big fiscal spending operation to help their economies to recover or, at least, to prevent rising unemployment and failing businesses from getting worse. Such spending recovery plans often are referred to as Keynesian economic stimulus plans—named for a twentieth-century English economist, John Maynard Keynes. In an article entitled "The Comeback Keynes," appearing in the October 23, 2008, issue of *TIME* magazine, Robert Lucas, who won a Nobel Prize for developing the theory of rational expectations that became a foundation for the belief that free markets provide the solution to any of our economic problems, is quoted as saying, "I guess everyone is a Keynesian in a foxhole."

In the early 1970s, however, the oil price spike by the Organization of Petroleum Exporting Countries (OPEC) led to extraordinarily high rates of inflation. What then was interpreted incorrectly as the "Keynesian" solution to this inflation problem did not appear to work. Instead, it seemed to induce a period of "stagflation"—a period in which both unemployment and prices were rising simultaneously. The failure of what was then called Keynesian anti-inflation policy, plus the public dissatisfaction with the Vietnam War, added to the general public's distrust of U.S. government policies. This revolt against big-government policies captured the public's imagination and opened up space for those who advocated a philosophy to get big government out of the way.

Accordingly, since the 1970s, economists and government policymakers have buried and almost forgotten Keynes's economic ideas and philosophy. Led by Milton Friedman and his colleagues at the University of Chicago, the ideas of the economics profession were recaptured by a free market, laissez-faire ideology. The public and government policymakers were educated in the classical economic ideas that only two things had to be done to promote economic progress and prosperity: (1) end the era of big government by reducing taxation to a bare minimum so that government had no money to spend on "lavish" programs, and (2) liberalize markets from all the government rules and regulations that had been installed by Franklin Roosevelt's New Deal administration. This alleged desirability of small government and unfettered markets was embraced by politicians, such as President Ronald Reagan in the United States and Prime Minister Margaret Thatcher in the United Kingdom.

No one was a greater advocate for freeing financial markets from all forms of government regulation than Alan Greenspan, the chairman of the Federal Reserve System (the Fed) from 1987 to 2006. During his reign at the Fed, the public and politicians treated Greenspan as if he could do no wrong. In testimony before congressional committees over the years, in language so oblique that it was hard to comprehend, Greenspan appeared to explain the inevitability of prosperity that would result from an unregulated, sophisticated financial system. And during his tenure as the chairman of the Federal Reserve Board of Governors, the U.S. economy did seem to be in a perpetual mode of low rates of inflation and significant economic growth—although, in hindsight, we recognize that much of the economic growth and prosperity was due mainly to the dot-com bubble of the 1990s, followed by a housing bubble in the first years of the twenty-first century. Currently, many "experts" now blame Greenspan for our problems, arguing that the cause of these "bubbles" was the easy-money and low-interest policy pursued by the Fed during Greenspan's tenure.

Nevertheless, while Greenspan was chairman, he was so persuasive that whether a Republican or a Democrat occupied the White House, the presidential administration endorsed Greenspan's idea of the efficiency of free markets. In fact, in his 1996 State of the Union address, President Bill Clinton announced that "the era of big government has ended."

Despite this optimism about a strong economy and small government, it should now be obvious that as a result of several decades of deregulation of markets, which Greenspan championed, and smaller government spending programs (except for military expenditures), both the United States and the global economy are enmeshed in the greatest economic crisis since the Great Depression.

In an amazing *mea culpa* testimony before the House Committee on Oversight and Government Reform on October 23, 2008, Alan Greenspan admitted that he had overestimated the ability of free financial markets to self-correct and had entirely missed the possibility that deregulation could unleash such a destructive force on the economy. In his prepared testimony discussing the financial crisis, Greenspan stated:

> This crisis, however, has turned out to be much broader than anything I could have imagined....[T]hose of us who had looked to the self-interest of lending institutions to protect

shareholder's equity (myself especially) are in a state of shocked disbelief....In recent decades, a vast risk management and pricing system has evolved, combining the best insights of mathematicians and finance experts supported by major advances in computer and communications technology. A Nobel Prize [in economics] was awarded for the discovery of the [free market] pricing model that underpins much of the advance in [financial] derivatives markets. This modern risk management paradigm held sway for decades. The whole intellectual edifice, however, [has] collapsed.

Under questioning by members of the congressional committee, Greenspan admitted that the events in financial markets forced him to reappraise his view that financial regulation is not required. He then stated: "I found a flaw in the model that I perceive is the critical functioning structure that defines how the world works. That's precisely the reason I was shocked....I still do not fully understand why it happened, and obviously to the extent that I figure it happened and why, I shall change my views."

A major purpose of this book is to explain in simple language the two major different economic ideas and philosophies regarding how a capitalist system operates and how these ideas suggest different explanations of the economic problems that arise over time. Moreover, I will explain how these alternative economic philosophies provide different rationales for solving the economic difficulties of the capitalist system in which we live. The first set of ideas goes by various names: classical or neoclassical economics, efficient market theory, and mainstream economic theory. The second analytical set of ideas is the liquidity and monetary analysis developed by John Maynard Keynes.

Winston Churchill once said, "No one pretends that democracy is perfect or all-wise. Indeed, it has been said that democracy is the worst form of government except all those other forms that have been tried from time to time." In a similar vein, during the Great Depression of the 1930s, Keynes developed an analytical framework designed to save what he clearly saw was the very imperfect entrepreneurial economic system that we call capitalism. Despite its imperfections, Keynes believed that capitalism was the best system humans have devised to achieve a civilized economic society. He recognized, however, that capitalism had two major faults: (1) its failure to provide persistent full employment for all those who want to work, and (2) its arbitrary and inequitable distribution of income and wealth. Until these faults were corrected, Keynes argued, the capitalist system could be extremely unstable and therefore subject to periods of economic booms that could often lead to catastrophic economic collapses.

Keynes's analysis explained why these two capitalist faults occur and how they can destabilize the economy. He argued that the government had a vital role to play to at least mitigate, if not completely remove, these flaws from the capitalist economic system in which we live. Keynes argued that, with properly designed government policies that cooperate and augment private initiatives, we could develop a stable, fully employed capitalist economy that would still enjoy the advantages of a market-oriented entrepreneurial system. These advantages, Keynes noted, are:

> of decentralization and of the play of self-interest.... But, above all, individualism, if it can be purged of its defects and its abuses, is the best safeguard of personal liberty in the sense that, compared with any other system, it greatly widens the field for the exercise of personal choice. It is also the best safeguard of the variety of life, which emerges precisely from this extended field of personal choice, and the loss of which is the greatest of all losses of the homogeneous or totalitarian state. For this variety preserves the traditions which embody the most secure and successful choices of former generations; it colours the present with the diversification of its fancy; and, being the handmaiden of experience as well as of tradition and of fancy, it is the most powerful instrument to better the future.[1]

If the government pursued Keynes's policy recommendations, and if we avoided major wars and civil dissent while we controlled population growth, then, Keynes believed, our grandchildren could inherit a world where starvation and poverty would be banished.

During the first quarter century after World War II, most governments in capitalist nations actively pursued the economic policies derived from Keynes's economic ideas. Stimulated by policies suggested by Keynes's ideas, per capita economic growth in the capitalist world occurred at a rate that had never been reached in the past nor matched since. The free world economy was starting to reach the civilized goal that Keynes envisioned. This postwar quarter century was an era of unsurpassed economic global prosperity, characterized by economist Irma Adelman as the "Golden Age of Economic Development...an era of unprecedented sustained economic growth in both developed and developing countries."[2]

This golden age of capitalist economic development raised the standard of living in noncommunist nations at such an unparalleled pace that by 1971 it has been recorded that even the Republican president Richard Nixon announced, "We are all Keynesians now."

In the chapters that follow, I develop the foundation of the "intellectual edifice" underlying classical economic ideas of the model that Greenspan believes in and that was propagated by classical economists and Nobel Prize winners such as Milton Friedman, Robert Lucas, Myron Scholes, and Robert Merton. I explain how these classical economic ideas led nations to repeat the errors that had led to the Great Depression. I also explain the differences between Keynes's analytical framework and the free "efficient market" analysis of the Chicago school that captured the mind of politicians and policymakers. I explain why Keynes's analysis leads to a different view regarding the role of government in stabilizing a market-oriented capitalist system and thereby avoiding the shipwrecks of financial crises.

I hope that, in my discussion of these ideas of classical economists versus Keynes, the reader is able to decide which is a more reasonable and applicable approach for understanding the cause of our current economic malady and the medicine necessary to cure the problem. I hope to convince the reader that incorporating the ideas of John Maynard Keynes into our entrepreneurial (capitalist) system will help rescue us from the economic havoc this economic and financial crisis that started in 2007 has caused. Perhaps if Greenspan reads this book and comprehends its message, then he will finally figure out what happened to cause the collapse of the classical intellectual edifice in which his mind resided and will change his views.

Chapter 2

IDEAS AND POLICIES THAT CREATED THE FIRST GLOBAL ECONOMIC CRISIS OF THE TWENTY-FIRST CENTURY

Those who cannot remember the past are condemned to repeat it.

—George Santayana

Although there were economic crises and unemployment problems in the nineteenth and early twentieth centuries, until the Great Depression that began in 1929, economists and politicians believed that booms and busts were nothing more than a natural business cycle. These economists believed that such natural phenomena were self-healing. Accordingly, until the Great Depression, most of these economists presumed that any economic downturn would be readily cured naturally by flexible prices operating in a free competitive market.

To the extent that downturns tended to persist, almost all economists of the time argued that this persistence was due to rigidities in wages and prices that are the result of monopolistic firms fixing prices, labor unions fixing wages, and/or government policies that intervened and limited the wage and price flexibility that would occur in competitive markets free of government interference.

In the United States, after a brief recession following World War I, the Roaring Twenties was a period of unbridled prosperity. In 1929, only 3.2 percent of American workers were unemployed. In 1920, the Dow Jones Stock Index stood at 63.9. During the years that followed, the New York Stock Exchange climbed to unprecedented highs. In 1929, the Dow Jones average peaked at 381.2, an increase of more than 500 percent in a little over eight years.

During the decade's stock market boom, people were able to buy stocks on "margin"—that is, for as little as 5 percent down and borrowing the rest—thereby leveraging[1] their stock position by a ratio of 19 to 1. In other words, they could borrow $19 for every $20 they invested in the stock market.[2]

By 1929, small individual investors, including blue-collar workers who had never invested in anything and knew little or nothing about the firms they invested in, were buying into the stock market on margin. Often these margin buyers relied on brokers or bankers to tell them where the profitable action was. Nevertheless, everyone in America seemed to be getting rich.[3]

Just a few days before the stock market crash of October 24, 1929, one of the most eminent classical economists of the time, Professor Irving Fisher of Yale University, told an audience that the market had reached a high plateau from which it could only go up. Then, suddenly, the bottom fell out. By June 1932, the Dow Jones had dropped by 89 percent from its 1929 high. It is said that Professor Fisher, who had put his money in what he believed in, lost between $8 million and $10 million—a vast sum in 1929—in this crash. The Great Depression had hit America.

From 1929 through 1933, the American economy went downhill. It seemed as if the economic system was enmeshed in a catastrophe from which it could not escape. Unemployment went from 3.2 percent in 1929 to almost 25 percent by 1933. One out of every four workers in the United States was unemployed by the time Franklin D. Roosevelt was inaugurated as president in March 1933. A measure of the standard of living of Americans, the real gross domestic product (GDP) per capita, fell by 52 percent between 1929 and 1933. This meant that, by 1933, the average American family was living on less than half of what it had earned in 1929. The American capitalist dream appeared to be shattered.

Many economic experts of those times still invoked classical economic theory to argue that the high level of unemployment in the United States was due to some fixity of wages and/or prices; and the depression would force workers and firms to accept lower prices. Consequently, the depression could not persist. The economy would soon right itself as long as the government did not interfere with the workings of a free competitive market system and workers and business firms accepted lower wages and prices for their productive efforts.

A wonderful example of this classical prescription is revealed in the memoirs of Herbert Hoover, the president of the United States from March 1929 to March 1933. Hoover had won praise as a kind and caring person due to his efforts to help feed the people of Europe, who were devastated by the effects of World War I. He obviously was a person who would try to alleviate a situation where humans experienced economic distress not of their own doing. In his memoir, Hoover noted that whenever he wanted to take positive action to end the depression and create jobs, his Treasury secretary, Andrew Mellon, always cautioned against government action and offered the same advice. "Mr. Mellon had only one formula. Liquidate labor, liquidate stocks, liquidate the farmer, liquidate real estate. It will purge the rottenness out of the system.... People will work harder, lead a more moral life."[4]

In England, however, the 1920s was a period of high unemployment: In most years, it exceeded 10 percent. It is, therefore, no wonder that English economists, and not American economists, were more concerned about the problem of chronic and persistent unemployment when the United States plunged into the Great Depression of the 1930s.

In England, the high unemployment rates of the 1920s had stimulated the eminent English economist John Maynard Keynes to try to explain why a capitalist economy such as the United Kingdom could suffer from such high rates of unemployment. Although Keynes was trained as a classical economist and even taught classical economic analysis at Cambridge before World War I, economic events after the war caused him to question the ideas of classical theory. Unlike the United States, Great Britain suffered from a great recession with double-digit unemployment rates throughout the decade of the 1920s except for one year, 1924, when the unemployment rate was estimated to be 9.4 percent. These facts forced Keynes to rethink the classical theory and its philosophy that claimed that workers' refusal to accept lower wages was the cause of unemployment. Over a period of 15 years, Keynes was able to develop an alternative to the classical set of ideas that he explained in his 1936 book, *The General Theory of Employment, Interest and Money*.

In this work, Keynes detailed the major economic faults of a money-using, market-oriented capitalist economic system and what policies could prevent these flaws while maintaining the benefits of a capitalist system. This analysis, Keynes believed, would replace the mainstream classical economic philosophy that free markets solved all economic problems, a philosophy that had dominated the thought of economists in England and the United States for almost two centuries.

On New Year's Day in 1935, Keynes wrote a letter to George Bernard Shaw in which he stated:

To understand my new state of mind...you have to know that I believe myself to be writing a book on economic theory which will largely revolutionize not I suppose at once but in the course of the next ten years the way the world thinks about economic problems. When my new theory has been duly assimilated and mixed with politics and feelings and passions, I cannot predict what the final upshot will be in its effect on actions and affairs, but there will be a great change and in particular the Ricardian Foundations of Marxism will be knocked away.

I can't expect you or anyone else to believe this at the present stage, but for myself I don't merely hope what I say. In my own mind I am quite sure.[5]

Thirteen months later, in February 1936, Keynes's book *The General Theory of Employment, Interest and Money* was published. Some of Keynes's innovative policy ideas did indeed impact government fiscal spending decisions during the Great Depression and World War II.

Roosevelt's New Deal and Keynes's Economics

By the time Roosevelt was elected in November 1932, many people realized that they were not experiencing a natural business cycle where the economy would bounce back if free markets were left to their own devices. When Roosevelt was inaugurated in March 1933, however, Keynes's ideas were not yet fully developed. Therefore, there was no systematic rationale to develop active governmental policies to replace the classical economic idea that free markets would ultimately in the long run reestablish full employment and prosperity for all members of society. At that time, the cleverest response to the classical argument that in the long run free markets would restore prosperity that Keynes had mustered was: "In the long run we will all be dead."[6]

On taking office, President Roosevelt did not have a complete and consistent plan to rescue the American economy from the Great Depression. In his inaugural speech in March 1933, Roosevelt could only assure the U.S. people that "The only thing we have to fear is fear itself." During its early days, the Roosevelt administration engaged in all sorts of experimental policies—some to stimulate the economy through spending, and some to change rules and regulations of the industrial environment.

In an open letter to the president, published in the *New York Times* on December 31, 1933, Keynes wrote:

Dear Mr. President,

You have made yourself the trustee for those in every country who seek to mend the evils of our condition by reasoned experiment within the framework of the existing social system.

If you fail, rational change will be gravely prejudiced throughout the world, leaving orthodoxy [classical theory] and revolution [Marxism] to fight it out.

But if you succeed, new and bolder methods will be tried everywhere, and we may succeed and we may date the first chapter of a new economic era from your accession to office.

Keynes went on to note that Roosevelt was engaged in a "double task, recovery and reform—recovery from the slump and the passage of those business and social reforms which are long overdue." Keynes warned, however, that "even wise and necessary reform may...impede complete recovery...[if it] will upset the confidence of business....And it will confuse the thought and aim of yourself and your Administration by giving you too much to think about all at once."

Similarly, in *The General Theory* (p. 162), Keynes warned that recovery from a slump can be jeopardized "[i]f the fear of a Labour Government or a New Deal depresses enterprise." In other words, *recovery must always be the first priority*, and any needed reforms must be packaged so as to encourage the enthusiasm of entrepreneurs and the public in general. It is not enough to advocate good and necessary reforms. One must be clever about how these reforms are packaged and presented to the public in order to gain their support.

From the very beginning, the Roosevelt administration moved out in many directions. Among the good and clever reforms the administration obtained were: guaranteeing bank deposits, refinancing many residential and farm mortgages, creating the Social Security system, creating the Securities and Exchange Commission to regulate financial asset markets, increasing labor's bargaining power, and mandating a reduction in working hours and an improvement in working conditions.

Recovery, however, was given priority above all these and other reforms. Roosevelt's administration engaged in significant government spending to create millions of jobs not only through what we today would call infrastructure investment (i.e., building bridges, schools, parks, roads, etc.), but also through environmental investment via the Tennessee Valley Authority and the Civilian Conservation Corps, as well as spending on the arts and culture, which resulted in the government hiring of actors such as Orson Welles, musicians, writers such as Clifford Odets, and artists such as Jackson Pollock and Willem de Kooning.

The New Deal was the name Roosevelt gave to the various stimulus programs that his administration initiated beginning in 1933 and ending in 1939. In an article entitled "Time for a New 'New Deal,'" published by the University of Texas Inequality Project in February 2009, Marshall Auerback indicated that Roosevelt's "New Deal" built or renovated 2,500 hospitals, 45,000 schools, 13,000 parks and playgrounds, 7,800 bridges, 700,000 miles of roads, many airfields, and planted billions of trees. The New Deal was also responsible for building New York's Lincoln Tunnel and Triborough Bridge, a significant portion of Chicago's Lakefront, the Montana state Capitol, the Cathedral of Learning in Pittsburgh, and other worthy projects that are still in use today. It also rebuilt the nation's rural school system.

In his first term in office, Roosevelt's spending to stimulate the economy resulted in deficits of $2 billion to $6 billion per year—sums that equaled between 2 and 5 percent of the GDP. By historical standards, the expansion of the economy between 1933 and 1936 was very robust. The 1936 real GDP—that is, adjusted for price level changes—was approximately as large as it had been in 1929, before the Great Depression had begun. Recovery seemed well in hand, although a larger population in 1936 meant that income per capita was still less than in 1929, and improvements in productivity plus the growth of the labor force meant that there was still significant unemployment. The official unemployment rate had fallen from approximately 25 percent in 1932 to 16 percent in 1936—although unofficial estimates indicate that the unemployment rate had fallen to 9 percent by 1936.[7]

Roosevelt's spending programs were often constrained by politicians who claimed that these large government spending deficits were "fiscally irresponsible." When Roosevelt entered the presidency, the national debt had totaled approximately 20 percent of the GDP. By 1936, the total government debt equaled 40 percent of the GDP. In that year, some economic experts were publicly stating that, if such reckless deficit spending continued, it would bankrupt the nation. Moreover, some argued that the government had already done enough by "pump priming" the increased demand for the products of industry.

Roosevelt recognized the power of this pump-priming argument as well as the fear of a large national debt causing the nation to become bankrupt. To show his determination to end such deficits and avoid national bankruptcy, Roosevelt in essence accepted the idea that need for "pump priming" by the federal government was over. Just prior to the 1936 November election, Roosevelt submitted to Congress a budget for fiscal year 1937 that was projected to halve the deficit, primarily by cutting government spending.

Roosevelt was reelected in a landslide, but the result of his 1937 fiscal-year austerity budget was a deep decline of almost 10 percent in real GDP through the first quarter of 1938. "Fiscally responsible" government policies in the 12 months of 1937 had undone what 4 years of deficits had achieved in creating jobs and significantly improving the economy. Obviously, this historical evidence indicates that priming the pump and then stopping a recovery program before full employment is achieved is not sufficient.

By comparison, President Barack Obama has talked about his stimulus plan jump-starting the economy. Obviously, in the twenty-first century, more people are aware how a jump-start causes an automobile to start to run; fewer understand how pump priming gets a well pump to work. Nevertheless, both the pump-priming and jump-starting comparisons imply that once some stimulus to the economy is applied, the economy apparently can recover on its own without further help from government. Will the same situation occur if the Obama administration just jump-starts the economy rather than pursuing a recovery program until full employment is achieved?

By mid-1938, Roosevelt restarted large deficit spending on both public works and the beginning of rearmament for possible war. By 1940, the GDP was 63 percent larger than it had been when Roosevelt took office in 1933, GDP per capita had increased by 55 percent, and the official unemployment rate had dropped below 10 percent. It is estimated that the average rate of economic growth during Roosevelt's New Deal years (1933–1940) exceeded 5 percent per annum, despite the 1937 recession pulling down this average.

Roosevelt was elected for a third term in November 1940, and, in 1941, the United States was plunged into war. Fears of an escalating national debt were abandoned. The important thing was to win the war and defeat the enemy, not to limit the size of the national debt. Annual budget deficits of between $20 billion and

$55 billion were incurred (equal to 14 to 31 percent of GDP) during the war years, while the GDP jumped from $114 billion to $221 billion. By the end of World War II, the national debt was equal to 119 percent of the GDP, and the unemployment rate had fallen below 2 percent.

The huge deficits of a world war not only defeated the enemy but also reestablished true prosperity and full employment in the United States. These facts validated Keynes's idea that when the economy suffers from severe recession or depression because private sector buyers are refusing to spend money on the goods and services that industry can produce, the government not only has the obligation to spend, but it can spend whatever is necessary to increase the demand for goods and services produced by private enterprise sufficiently to achieve full employment and prosperity, regardless of the size of the resulting national deficit. The rationale for Keynes's idea that government can always act as the spender of last resort to restore prosperity is explained in chapter 4.

Early Post–World War II Perversion of "Keynesian" Economics

Unfortunately, early post–World War II economists, who often called themselves "Keynesians," failed to comprehend the logically consistent innovative theoretical analysis and philosophy laid down by Keynes. Accordingly, what was called Keynesianism in professional economic writings and popular economic textbooks of the day was, as I explain in chapter 9, nothing more than a modernized version of the pre-Keynesian, nineteenth-century free market classical argument. This perverse "Keynesian" analysis, just like nineteenth- and early twentieth-century classical theory, put the blame for unemployment on rigid high wages and monopoly pricing. The only difference between the arguments is that the former had been larded over with some Keynesian terminology and policy prescriptions.

In this corruption of Keynes's argument, unemployment was ultimately due to three things:

1. Unions and workers refusing to accept a lower wage that would create jobs for all workers who wanted to work, a wage that economists call the market clearing wage.
2. Governments dictating a minimum wage that is greater than that hypothetical market clearing wage.
3. Monopolists demanding a price for their products that was higher than what a competitive market price would be.

Of course, classical theorists had always argued that if workers refused to accept a market-determined wage—no matter how low it is—and/or if monopolists charged too high a price for their products, then the operation of free competitive markets would be impaired. The unwillingness of workers to let wages fall and of monopolists to fix and maintain prices at a noncompetitive high level, classical theory claimed, would prevent a "free" market from working its magic. In a typical blame-the-victim-for-the-problem argument, classical theory always suggested that any persistent unemployment is due to the truculence of workers refusing to accept a market-determined wage rate that would ensure full employment.

If this perverted view was correct, the solution to the unemployment problem might be to break up monopolies, destroy the unions, and get the government out of the business of legislating minimum wages. These perverse Keynesians did not recommend such solutions. Rather, they advocated increasing spending sufficiently to expand demand in the face of the rigidity of wages and prices, until even at these high fixed wages and prices, the market would buy everything presented for sale.

Keynes, however, recognized that unemployment increased significantly more in a depression than in prosperous boom times, and therefore it was not workers' truculence that caused unemployment. Keynes noted that "[l]abour is not more truculent in a depression than in a boom—far from it. Nor is its physical productivity less. These facts from experience are a *prima facie* ground for questioning the adequacy of the classical analysis"[8] that asserted that workers facing increasing unemployment rates will, nevertheless, be stubbornly defiant of the free market's authority to develop a wage that will assure all who want to work can obtain employment.

Keynes argued that the fundamental cause of unemployment was *not* due to the fixity of wages and prices preventing a free market from operating to ensure full employment. Instead of laying the blame for unemployment on the rigidity of wages and prices, Keynes's novel idea was that when unemployment occurs, the cause involves the fact that savers are demanding increased liquidity from the financial assets that they use to store their savings. The problem of unemployment was to be found in the operation of financial markets and the motives of savers to save.

Given this argument, it should be obvious that these early postwar Keynesian explanations were, in fact, incompatible with Keynes's analysis even though the economists exploited the name of "Keynesian economics" to sell their argument.

Need for Regulation of Banking and Financial Markets

After the U.S. stock market crash of October 1929, one out of every five banks in the United States failed. The public and politicians believed that a basic cause of the Great Depression was the financial market speculation engaged in and encouraged by the banks in the 1920s. Beginning in 1932, the U.S. Senate Committee on Banking and Currency held hearings on the possible causes of the crash. These hearings suggested that in the early part of the century, individual investors were seriously hurt by banks whose self-interest lay in underwriting and promoting sales of securities that benefited only the banks, not the buyers of these securities. The hearings concluded that a major cause of the 1929 stock market crash was the fact that banks, in the 1920s, significantly increased their underwriting activities and their promotions of security purchases to individual investors. Consequently, in 1933, Congress passed the Glass-Steagall Act, a legislative reform involving the banking system and organized securities markets.

The Glass-Steagall Act banned banks from underwriting and promoting the sale of securities. Financial institutions had to choose to be either simple bank lenders *or* underwriters (investment bankers, brokerage firms). The act instituted a legal barrier between these two financial operations and gave the Federal Reserve more control over banking activities. (As will be explained later, when the Glass-Steagall Act was repealed in 1999, large-scale promotion of bank underwriting and sales of mortgage-backed and other securities helped precipitate the stock market decline of 2008 and the financial crisis of that time.)

As a result of the Glass-Steagall Act, for several decades, bank-originated mortgage loans were not resalable. The mortgage debt instruments were illiquid assets. Originating bank lenders knew that the bank would have to carry the mortgage loan debt security on its books over its entire life. If the borrower defaulted, the lender bank would bear the costs of foreclosure and possible loss. Thus, the originating bank lender thoroughly investigated the three Cs of each borrower—collateral, credit history, and character—before making the mortgage loan. Moreover, the mortgage lender typically required a significant down payment as a cushion in case the borrower ran into difficult economic times and had to default, despite its high rating for the three Cs.

Deregulating the Banking System and Financial Markets: The Return of Free Market Ideas

By the 1970s, the perverted version of Keynes's argument was beginning to lose its luster. This decline created a vacuum in public discussions of economics. Economist Milton Friedman quickly moved in, actively promoting the classical economic philosophy in the public forum. Friedman argued that if we reduced the size of big government and removed the rules and regulations instituted during the Roosevelt administration that limited the play of free markets, the economy would prosper in ways that it could not with big government interference.

Deregulation of banking activities began in the 1970s in the United States, when brokerage firms began offering money market, higher-interest, checkwriting accounts that competed with traditional banking business. The general public applauded this small invasion of brokers into the banking business; people could earn a slightly higher return on these (uninsured) money market deposits than they were earning on deposits in regulated banks, whose deposits were insured by a governmental agency.

In the 1980s, the Fed reinterpreted the Glass-Steagall Act to allow banks to engage in securities underwriting activities that contributed up to 5 percent of gross revenues and to compete in securities markets with the brokerage firms that had invaded their checking account business. In 1987, the Fed allowed banks to handle significantly larger—but still limited—underwriting activities, including those of mortgage-backed securities, despite the objections of Paul Volker, then the Fed chairman. When Alan Greenspan became chair of the Federal Reserve Board of Governors later in 1987, he favored further bank deregulation to help U.S. banks compete with foreign banks, which are often universal banks that can act as investment banks and take equity stakes.

In 1996, the Fed permitted bank holding companies to own investment banking affiliates, which can contribute up to 25 percent of total revenue of the holding company. Finally, in 1999, after 12 attempts in 25 years, Congress, with the support of President Clinton, repealed the Glass-Steagall Act. In an article in the *Wall Street Journal* on October 25, 1999—a few days before Congress repealed the act—Republican senator Phil Gramm is quoted as telling a Citigroup lobbyist to "get [Citigroup co-chairman] Sandy Weill on the phone right now. Tell him to call the White House and get [them] moving" or else Congress would not repeal the act. Soon after Gramm's warning, the president did support the act's repeal. Shortly after Congress repealed the act, Robert Rubin (a former investment banker), who had been a secretary of the Treasury in the Clinton administration, accepted a top job at Citigroup.

Once Glass-Steagall was repealed, there were no legal constraints between loan origination and underwriting activities. An apparently unlimited profit incentive was created for mortgage originators to search out potential homebuyers (including subprime ones, i.e., borrowers who would not normally meet the three Cs of old-style mortgage bank lenders) and provide them with mortgages. The originators could then profitably sell these mortgages, usually within 30 days, to an underwriter, or act as underwriters themselves to sell the mortgages to the public. Underwriters would combine many mortgages into a mortgage-backed security (MBS) and sell tranches (i.e., prioritized claims of a MBS) to various members of the public. These loan originators had little to fear from borrower defaults as long as borrowers were able to make their first monthly mortgage payment.

When the mortgage originators could not find enough qualified borrowers for mortgages, the incentive to earn income encouraged them to find less qualified (i.e., subprime) borrowers in order to continue reselling mortgages and collecting origination fees. In many cases, mortgage originators perpetrated fraud in providing information (or misinformation) about borrowers in order to qualify them for a mortgage. Eventually the mortgage borrowers, especially the subprime ones and those who had obtained mortgages using false information, began to default on their debt-servicing obligations. Of course, most of these defaulting mortgage borrowers probably would not have passed the three Cs test of the old-time mortgage bank lender.

These subprime mortgages were originated and sold to investment bank underwriters, who combined and packaged them with other mortgages and created financial assets called CDOs (collateralized debt obligations), SIVs (structured investment vehicles), and other esoteric financial vehicles whose earnings were derived from the underlying mortgages. The underwriters then sold tranches in these derivatives to unwary pension funds, local and state revenue funds, individual investors, and other banks, domestic or overseas. Investors were not aware of the composition of the mortgages that were to generate the cash flow for these derivatives. Instead, led on by the high ratings these complex financial securities received from private rating agencies, investors believed they were safe investments.

Investors spent vast sums buying these mortgage-backed financial securities despite the fact that no one was sure of what actual real assets were pledged as collateral against them. This process of taking a mixture of heterogeneous illiquid assets (e.g., nonmarketable residential mortgages) and packaging them into complex financial securities that were then diced and sliced and sold to investors is called "securitization." How this securitization process led to creating a credit crisis of epidemic proportions in the global economy is explained in chapter 6.

Since the beginning of the twenty-first century, this process of securitizing mortgages helped to finance the housing bubble that pushed housing prices to historic highs by early 2006. In a December 14, 2007, piece, *New York Times* op-ed writer and Nobel Prize winner Paul Krugman defined the bubble as a situation where the price of housing exceeded a "normal ratio" relative to rents or incomes. By December 2007, foreclosure proceedings were accelerating, and the stock of vacant housing was increasing dramatically. This put pressure on the prices of existing occupied houses, and housing prices began to fall rapidly. In his article, Krugman did not suggest any remedies that government could take to relieve the distress caused by the deflating housing bubble. He wrote that the housing market would solve the problem by deflating housing prices until they would fall by approximately 30 percent to restore a normal ratio relative to people's income. Krugman's 30 percent estimate of housing price decline implied that the total value of people's equity in their homes would decline by approximately $6 trillion from the December 2007 value. As measured by the Case/Shiller housing price index, in October 2008, housing prices had declined approximately only 23 percent from their 2006 peak.

With such a steep decline in housing prices, many homeowner borrowers found themselves with negative equity; their outstanding mortgages exceeded the market price that could be obtained if the homes were sold—an insolvency problem. Krugman indicated that there is no quick fix of this negative equity problem, and it will "take years" for the market to clean up the housing mess.

In many U.S. states, mortgages are nonrecourse loans (i.e., after default and foreclosure, the borrower is not responsible for any difference between the outstanding mortgage balance and the lower sale price at foreclosure). If Krugman's 30 percent house value decline estimate is fairly accurate, as many as 10 million households could end up with negative equity and will have a strong incentive to default. Millions of homeowners will lose their homes in foreclosure proceedings, and investors in mortgage-backed securities will incur large losses.

Home Owners' Loan Corporation

A study of history can provide a clue about how to solve today's housing bubble problem. The Roosevelt administration's handling of the housing default crisis of the 1930s suggests a precedent for dealing with the U.S. housing bubble distress that began in 2007. In 1933, the United States Congress passed the Home Owners Refinancing Act, which created the Home Owners' Loan Corporation (HOLC). The primary function of the HOLC was to refinance homes to prevent foreclosures and to bail out mortgage-holding banks.

The HOLC was a tremendous success. The program made one million low-interest loans that often extended the payoff period of the original loan, thereby significantly reducing the monthly payments to amounts homeowners could afford. In case a homeowner could not afford the mortgage on any reasonable terms, the HOLC took title to the property and rented it to the former homeowner on a month-to-month basis that he or she could afford. In this way, the HOLC was assured that the home would not be left vacant, subject to decay and possible vandalism. When the HOLC could sell the house to another family who would move in, the renter had to move out. In its years of operation from 1933 to 1951, the HOLC not only paid all its bills but also made a small profit.

Another measure the government might undertake is to set up a government agency to take nonperforming mortgage loans and other so-called toxic assets off the books of private balance sheets, thereby removing the threat of insolvency for those who took positions in the mortgage-backed securities market after being misled by rating agencies. Doing so would prevent further sell-offs that would cause financial distress in all financial markets.

History again provides some proof that such measures can avert an economic crisis. For example, the Resolution Trust Corporation, set up in 1989 by the U.S. government, did remove nonperforming mortgage loans from the balance sheets of building societies after the 1980s savings and loan crisis, thereby preventing further financial damage.

Unfortunately, when the housing bubble mess first became obvious in 2007, Congress did not act promptly to create the necessary government agencies to help clean it up. Washington's initial reaction was to leave the solution to the market, which Krugman had suggested would take years. Moreover the "leave it to the market" solution has caused, and will continue to cause, collateral damage to many innocent economic casualties (e.g., homeowners in neighborhoods where foreclosures are prevalent and workers and firms in construction and related industries).

Moral of the History of the Great Depression

Since the current economic crisis is aptly described as the most serious economic problem since the Great Depression, the lessons learned from studying the history of the depression era should be seen as to how they apply to the current situation. The government has an important role in ensuring a recovery that is as quick as possible from our current recession by promoting increased market demand for the products of business firms, thereby creating profit opportunities that will encourage enterprises to create more job opportunities. This role requires the government to reject the idea that all that may be necessary is a little pump priming or jump-starting to get the recovery going. A fiscal spending policy that ensures strong and persistent recovery with less worry about the size of the deficit and total government debt incurred is essential.

Once a strong recovery is in place, the administration must decide what reforms are necessary in terms of rules and regulations that limit activities in the marketplace to those that create a civilized society.

Chapter 3

READING TEA LEAVES TO "KNOW" THE FUTURE

Classical Theory's Ideas about a Capitalist System

Since biblical times, humans have tried to understand the world around them and what caused things to happen. In general, the human mind believes that there must be a cause for any event we observe.

For most of the history of humankind, it was believed that the design of God or the gods was the cause of anything that happened in the world of experience. Beginning in the seventeenth century, however, some philosophers believed that explanations of events that one observed could be developed on the basis of reasoning of the mind rather than religious belief. This was the beginning of the intellectual movement historians call the Enlightenment or the Age of Reason, where order and regularity were seen to come from the human analysis of observed phenomena. The power of reason was not in the possession of truth but in its acquisition.

Any understanding of the world as humans perceive it will, to some extent, always be the creation of the human mind. Reasoning involves the mind creating a theory to explain what people observe happening around them. For example, Sir Isaac Newton saw an apple fall from the bough of a tree to the ground. He developed the theory of gravity to explain why apples always fall to the ground. Charles Darwin developed the theory of evolution to explain the different species inhabiting Earth. And Albert Einstein provided the general theory of relativity to explain a time-space continuum. Although in today's society there are people of religious belief who still attribute certain events that happen to the will of God, most of society believes that understanding comes with the development of scientific theories.

A theory is the way humans describe real-world observations on the basis of a model that starts with a few axioms. An axiom is an assumption accepted as a universal truth that does not need to be proven. From this axiomatic foundation, the theorist uses the laws of logic to reach conclusions that explain what we observe in the world of experience. All theories are generally accepted in some tentative fashion. Theories are never conclusively established.

Economic theory is an analytical device in which economic theorists build a model by starting with some axioms that they accept as self-evident truths. The tools of logical deduction are then used to reach one or more conclusions. These conclusions are then presented to the public as the explanation of economic events that are occurring in the world of experience. The theory can then be used to suggest the cure for any real-world economic problems.

There are two fundamentally different economic theories that attempt to explain the operation of a capitalist economy: classical economic theory and Keynes's liquidity theory of an entrepreneurial economy. The first theory, classical economic theory, sometimes is referred to as the theory of efficient markets, neoclassical economic theory, or mainstream economic theory. The mantra of this analytical system is that free markets can cure any economic problem that may arise while government interference in free markets always causes economic problems. In other words, interventionist government economic policy is the problem while the free market is the solution.

Classical theory's logical deduction results in a laissez-faire philosophy where government should never interfere with the operation of a free market economy.

The second theory, Keynes's liquidity theory of an entrepreneurial economy, demonstrates that government has the capacity to cure, *with the cooperation of private industry and households*, economic flaws inherent in the operation of a money-using, market-oriented capitalist economy.

In this chapter we explain the axiomatic foundation of classical theory and evaluate the usefulness of its view of what policies, if any, can help the economy to recover as rapidly as possible from our current economic and financial market crisis and ensure a civilized, prosperous capitalist economy for ourselves and our children.

In chapter 4 we make a similar evaluation of Keynes's theory and ideas regarding the operation of our capitalist system. The comparison of these alternate theories of how our economic system operates will aid readers in judging the various economic policies our government leaders advocate to solve the important economic problems of our times.

The best way to evaluate any economic theory is to consider theorists as if they are magicians. Just as professional magicians rarely drop the deck of cards while performing a card trick, theorists rarely make logical errors in moving from axioms to conclusions. Today's mainstream economic theorists are proficient at creating complex mathematical models that reach the policy conclusion that government interference prevents free markets from solving all economic problems.

In the absence of any mistake in logic, the axioms of any theory determine its conclusions. Accordingly, in order to evaluate the relevance of any policy derived from an economic model, one should carefully examine the axioms that form the foundation of the model. If the axioms underlying the model have been explicitly or implicitly accepted, then the policies derived from the model cannot be criticized. In fact, of course, most laypersons and even many economists are completely unaware of the implausible axioms loaded into the foundation of today's highly complex classical mathematical models of the economy that are used to manage risks and forecast the economic future.

Before accepting the conclusions of any economist's model as correctly descriptive and therefore applicable to the money-using, market-oriented entrepreneurial system in which we live, caring people, investment bankers, business executives, and government officials should always examine and be prepared to criticize the basic axioms of the model. Are the fundamental axioms—those that are used as a foundation upon which the economic analysis is built—applicable to the economic world in which we live? If the axioms cannot be accepted as realistic representations of our world, then the audience must reject the policy conclusions derived from the theory.

Let us begin, therefore, by examining the basic "universal truths" that underlie mainstream classical theorists' policy pronouncements regarding the efficacy of free markets to solve our economic problems.

Classical Theory's Way of Dealing with an Uncertain Future

Time is a device for preventing everything from happening at once. Economic decisions made today will have outcomes that can be evaluated only days, months, or even years in the future. The basic—but not only—difference between these classical theories and the Keynes theory is how they treat knowledge about future outcomes of today's decisions. In essence, the classical theory presumes that, by one method or another, decision makers today can, and do, possess knowledge about the future. Thus, the only economic problem that markets have to solve is the allocation of resources to meet the most valuable outcomes for today and for future dates.

The Keynes liquidity theory, in contrast, presumes that decision makers "know" that they do not, and cannot, know the future outcome of certain crucial economic decisions made today. Thus, this theory explains how the capitalist economic system creates institutions that permit decision makers to deal with an uncertain future while making allocative decisions and then to sleep at night.

Advocates of classical economics believe that free markets are efficient. In a classical efficient market, it is presumed that there are large numbers of rational decision makers who, before making a purchase or sales decision, collect and analyze *reliable information* both on the probability of events that have already occurred and on the *probability of events that will occur in the future*. In an efficient market, it is assumed that this important information about the past and the future is readily available to decision makers and that, on the basis of this information, decision makers make optimal choices.

Lawrence Summers, former secretary of the Treasury and President Obama's economic advisor, has stated that "the ultimate social functions [of efficient markets are] spreading risks, guiding the investment of scarce capital, and processing and disseminating the information possessed by diverse traders.... [P]rices will always reflect fundamental values.... The logic of efficient markets is compelling."[1]

Decisions that are made today will produce outcomes at some time in the future. Since most produced goods and services take some time to fabricate, business firms must make hiring and production decisions today to produce output that only can be sold, delivered, and paid for at some future date. Furthermore, business firms planning to invest in new plant and equipment have to evaluate the potential profits this investment will make by producing output over the useful life of this equipment. This "useful life" often extends years and even decades into the future.

Even purchases of consumer goods and services to be delivered later today or at some scheduled future date (or dates) require self-interested buyers to evaluate the utility of such purchases to them at that future time of delivery. If markets are to be efficient and truly provide the social functions that Summers claims for free markets, then both buyers and sellers *must know* the resulting value of all the possible outcomes that will occur in the future.

For financial markets such as the stock and bond markets to be efficient, people must "know" future revenues and profits to be obtained from the underlying plant and equipment business firms own. If you believe in efficient financial markets, then these future revenues and profits are Summers's "fundamentals" that determine today's market prices of securities traded in financial markets.

In previous centuries, economists such as Adam Smith, David Ricardo, John Stuart Mill, and Alfred Marshall assumed that market participants possessed complete information about the future and therefore that, in a free market, all participants would always make the correct decisions that represented their own best interests. Obviously an assumption that the future is already known is preposterous. Nevertheless, this idea underlies the belief of Alan Greenspan (cited in chapter 1) that the self-interest of lending institutions in a free market would lead management to undertake transactions that protect shareholders' equity. This idea also underlies the antitax, rhetorical question of Ronald Reagan: "Why should some bureaucrats in Washington know better than you on how to spend your income?" After all, if you "know" the future, you should be able to protect yourself and your family against any possible adverse future events and, by your investment decisions in financial market securities, ensure yourself sufficient retirement income to live comfortably for the rest of your life. Clearly if you know the future and act in your own self-interest, you do not need Washington bureaucrats to take your tax money to provide you, and all other retirees, with a basic Social Security retirement income no matter what happens. In the classical theory world where everyone knows the future, all self-interested people can better plan for their future retirement income than some governmental Social Security managers can.

All of today's classical efficient market models are based on some variants of this presumption that the future is known. Having solved, by assumption, the problem of knowing the value of future outcomes, classical theory asserts that the only significant economic problem is to ensure that today's economic decisions allocate resources that produce outcomes in the future that are most highly valued when the outcome occurs. In other words, for classical theorists, the only problem is a resource allocation one. If we accept the assumption that self-interested decision makers reliably "know" the future, then their decisions made in a free, competitive marketplace will result in the best allocation of resources possible.

Economists have spent many years working out theoretical models of the operation of efficient markets. Each model may have a slightly different mechanism for describing how today's economic decision makers know future outcomes. For example, the mathematically sophisticated Arrow-Debreu general equilibrium model (Kenneth Arrow and Gerard Debreu are both Nobel Prize recipients) is an elaboration of a nineteenth-century efficient market model called the Walrasian general equilibrium model. These general equilibrium analytical models are the base upon which are built today's complex mathematical computer economic models used at the most prestigious institutions, such as the Council of Economic Advisors and the Federal Reserve.

This general equilibrium analysis presumes that markets exist today that permit participants to buy and sell all the products and services that will be delivered at each date in the future. Thus, at the initial instant of time, it is presumed that all market participants can decide to enter into transactions for the purchases and sales of all products, services, and financial assets not only for delivery today but for delivery for all future dates *until the end of time*. In its extreme conceptualization, this complex mathematical model implies that all the decision makers today not only know what goods and services they are going to demand and/or supply in the market today, tomorrow, and every future date for the rest of their lives; they also "know" what their grandchildren, great-grandchildren, and all future heirs will want to buy and sell decades and centuries into the future. Therefore, they will today also sign buy and/or sell contracts for all future dates for these future generations.

The high level of mathematics and abstraction of this model of classical theory enables its theorists to bury its impossible axiomatic foundation: that today's decision makers know the future until the end of time.

Many of today's mainstream classical economists recognize that the Arrow-Debreu presumption of the existence of a complete set of markets for every conceivable good and service for every future date until the end of time is impossible. Nevertheless, they still believe in the efficiency of free markets while recognizing that, in the real world, there cannot be a complete set of markets for all future dates. To salvage their efficient market conclusions, these economists instead assume that today's market participants possess "rational expectations" regarding all future possible outcomes of any decision made today. This theory of rational expectations (developed by Nobel Prize winner Robert Lucas) asserts that somehow today's decision makers possess statistically reliable information regarding the probabilities that govern all conceivable future outcomes.

From a technical point of view, statisticians require an analyst to draw a random sample from a population in order to calculate reliable probability information about that population's characteristics.

Accordingly, to obtain reliable information regarding the future of all possible market outcomes, one should obtain a sample taken from the future. Then today's rational decision makers can analyze this sample from the future in order to calculate statistically reliable information about the probability distribution governing all future outcomes. If that statistically reliable information about the future can be obtained readily from this sample drawn from the future, then the decision makers can reduce uncertainty about prospective outcomes to a future of actuarial certainties expressed as objective probabilistic risks.

Since drawing a sample from the future is not possible, efficient market theorists presume that probabilities calculated from already existing past and current market data are equivalent to drawing a sample from markets that will exist in the future. In other words, calculations of probabilistic risks from the past statistics are assumed to be equivalent to calculations that would be obtained if a sample from the future could be obtained.

The presumption that data samples from the past are equivalent to data samples from the future is called *the ergodic axiom*. Those who invoke this ergodic assertion argue that economics can be a "hard science" like physics or astronomy *only* if the ergodic axiom is part of the economist's model. In 1968, for example, Paul Samuelson, who is thought to be the originator of post–World War II Keynesianism and who won the Nobel Prize in Economics in 1970, wrote that if economists hope to remove economics from the realm of history and move it into the realm of science, they must impose the "ergodic hypothesis."

This ergodic presumption is the essential foundation of classical efficient market theory. Unless the future is known, today's market participants cannot make decisions that the future will prove were efficient. But as I explain in chapter 4, Keynes rejected this ergodic axiom in developing his analysis of how a capitalist system operated in the real world when crucial decisions have to be made.

Ergodicity is an esoteric statistical concept; simply put, whenever analysts invoke the ergodic axiom, they are proclaiming that statistical samples drawn from past or current market data are equivalent to drawing samples from future market data. In other words, these analysts assume that the future is merely the statistical shadow of the past. If—and only if—this axiom is accepted as a universal truth will calculating probability distributions (risks) on the basis of historical market data be statistically equivalent to drawing and analyzing samples from the future.

It should not be surprising that all the highly complex computer models that investment bankers use as risk management tools to evaluate future risks on their current portfolio holdings of financial assets are based on a statistical analysis of historical market data. The statistical probabilities of risks that these complex mathematical models calculated from past experience resulted in enormous errors for evaluating future risks. These computer model results led to the downfall of the American investment banking industry in 2008.

Alan Greenspan has admitted that this collapse of the investment banking industry shocked him, but he "still does not understand why it happened." Given that Secretary of the Treasury Henry Paulson and the Congress in the fall of 2008 recognized the necessity for government to bail out all the Wall Street investment bankers, and that Wall Street bankers willingly admitted their need for such bailouts, it should be obvious that all the risk management computer models used in recent years failed to predict the disaster that happened to the balance sheets of Wall Street investment bankers in 2008. It is hoped that Greenspan will now understand why his intellectual "edifice" based on the ergodic axiom failed so spectacularly.

This assumption that the economy is governed by an ergodic process means that the future path of the economy is already predetermined and cannot be changed by human action today. As an example of how this ergodic axiom works in other spheres, consider that astronomers insist that the future path of the planets around the sun and the moon around Earth has been predetermined since the moment of the "Big Bang" beginning of the universe. Nothing humans can do can change the predetermined path of these heavenly bodies. This Big Bang astronomy theory means that the "hard science" of astronomy relies on the ergodic axiom to predict the future path of heavenly bodies. Consequently, by using past data obtained by observations regarding the speed and direction of heavenly bodies, astronomical scientists can accurately predict the time (usually within seconds) of when the next solar eclipse will be observable on Earth.

If this ergodic-based hard science of astronomy is applicable to predicting the predetermined path of heavenly bodies in our universe, then it should be obvious that the U.S. Congress cannot pass legislation that actually will prevent future solar eclipses from occurring, even if the purpose of such legislation is to obtain more sunshine on Earth to increase crop production. In a similar vein, if, as Samuelson claims, economics is a "hard science" based on the ergodic axiom, then Congress cannot pass a law preventing the next recession from occurring any more than it can prevent the next eclipse. It logically follows from basing a model on the ergodic assumption that there is nothing Congress can do to prevent unpleasant economic events that are already predetermined in the future path of the economy. The result is a belief in a laissez-faire nongovernment intervention policy as the only correct policy.

Efficient market theorists who believe themselves to profess a hard science must argue that Congress cannot pass legislation that permanently alters the predetermined future path of the economy. Logically consistent efficient market analysis suggests that active government economic policies that interfere with free markets create an external shock to the system. By an "external shock," the efficient theory economists mean that government policy is equivalent to throwing something into the predetermined path of the economy, pushing it temporarily off its path into one involving more unemployment, resource waste, and the like.

An analog to this external shock concept would be if we threw a pebble that hit a swinging pendulum. The pebble would produce an external shock that momentarily pushes the pendulum off its swinging path into a more erratic one. Unless we continued to throw more pebbles, the effect of the one-time pebble external shock would wear off, and the pendulum would soon return to its natural swinging path as the ergodic law of gravity reestablished control over it.

If markets are efficient and not constrained by onerous permanent government regulation and interference, the reaction of participants in these efficient markets to any external shock caused by government policies will move the economy back to its predetermined efficient path, just as the law of gravity would restore the pendulum swing after the external shock of being hit by a pebble. In other words, whenever government policies shock the economic system, action by rational market participants in a free market, in some unspecified time (i.e., the long run), will restore the system back to its predetermined efficient path by purging "the rottenness out of the system" (to use Andrew Mellon's elegant phraseology).

Thus, for example, it is often argued that the government creates unemployment in the private sector when it passes legislation that all workers are entitled to at least minimum wage that cannot be lowered even if unemployed workers are willing to work for less rather than starve. Similarly, if government passes legislation that protects and encourages unionization, the effect will be to push wages up so high that profit opportunities ultimately will be eliminated and unemployment of workers assured. Thus, it follows from classical theory that the market and not the government should decide what wage rate should be the minimum that workers receive. Consistency therefore would require arguing that government should never constrain the pay of top management but rather should leave it to the market to determine the value of managers.

In an article entitled "Faith and Reason in the Mathematics of the Credit Crunch," appearing in *Oxford Magazine* in the spring of 2008, the Oxford mathematician Jerome Ravitz wrote:

> The term faith is believed by these competent present observers to be relevant to the mathematics at the heart of the multi dimensional pyramid game that has led to our present [credit crunch] catastrophe. Combined with the corruption of quality and the abuse of uncertainty in mathematical models, blind faith in [classical] economics and mathematics forms the third element of the toxic mix that has enabled greed and irresponsibility to wreak their destructive way.... Mathematics first provided an enabling technology with computers, then with a plausible theorem it offered legitimation for runaway speculation and finally, with models of their value, risk and quality, it framed the quantitative specification of its fantasised products. Mathematics thereby became uniquely toxic, what Warren Buffett has called "weapons of mass destruction."

Classical Theorists versus Keynes on the Reality of Assumptions

If Keynes was alive today, he might have called this theory of efficient markets a case of "weapons of math destruction." Yet economist Robert Lucas has boasted that the axioms underlying classical economics are "artificial, abstract, patently unreal."[2] But like Samuelson, Lucas insists such unreal assumptions are the only scientific method of doing economics. Lucas insists that "progress in economic thinking means getting better and better abstract, analogue models, not better verbal observations about the real world." The rationale underlying this argument is that these unrealistic assumptions make the problem more tractable. With the aid of a computer, the analyst can then predict the future. Never mind that the prediction might be disastrously wrong.

Computer-based mathematical versions of classical efficient market theory involving thousands of variables and an equation for each variable have been put forth as a hard science description of our economic system that, at a point of time, simultaneously permits the determination of the price and output of every item that is traded in the economic system. For many economists, even identifying the fundamental axioms buried under all the mathematical debris is an impossible task. Moreover, the fact that computers can manipulate all that mathematics gives the results an aura of scientific truth. How can a computer printout be wrong?

In a 2009 article entitled "Probably Wrong—Misapplications of Probability and Statistics in Real Life Uncertainty," Oxford University's Peter Taylor and David Shipley of MAP Underwriting Agencies, Lloyd's of London, suggest why all these computer printouts are wrong. They write:

> There are lies, damned lies, and statistics....Probability and Statistics just don't feel right for many problems....They give the impression of allowing fairly for the eventualities...and then something unexpected happens....Those of a more pragmatic nature would want some measure of credibility such as the extent of applicability to a theory or a problem. In complex systems, the predictability that is so successful in the controlled worlds of the lab and engineering has not worked and yet theories claiming predictability have misled policy makers and continue to do so....We may even have to own up to not having an appropriate model at all, surely a modern-day heresy.

Taylor and Shipley argue that we should learn from the current economic and financial crisis:

> As investors, never trust a manager who says he has a superior mathematical model....As managers leave room in your business model for the unexpected....As regulators focus on management's ability to understand real risk exposure, rather than

the comfort blanket of a model....As modellers, encourage critical awareness that the model may not represent all the relevant mechanisms for the process under consideration.

In the introduction to his bestselling book *Against the Gods*, which deals with the questions of relevance of risk management techniques on Wall Street, Peter L. Bernstein writes on page 6: "The story that I have to tell is marked all the way through by a persistent tension between those who assert that the best decisions are based on quantification and numbers, determined by the [statistical] patterns of the past, and those who based their decisions on more subjective degrees of belief about the uncertain future. This is a controversy that has never been resolved."

One hopes that the empirical evidence of the collapse of all the models designed by those "masters of the economic universe" who have dominated Wall Street machinations for the past three decades has at least created doubt regarding the applicability to our economic world of classical theory, despite all its quantification and mathematical garb. Even Alan Greenspan seems to be having second thoughts, although he still has not completely changed his tune.

John Maynard Keynes's ideas support Bernstein's latter group, who base decisions on subjective beliefs. Keynes specifically argued that the uncertainty of the economic future cannot be resolved by looking at statistical patterns of the past. Keynes believed that today's economic decisions regarding spending and saving depend on people's subjective degree of belief regarding possible future events. In the next chapter, I discuss Keynes's ideas, which provide an alternative to the classical efficient market theory mind-set. My aim is to convince the reader that Keynes's ideas are more applicable to our capitalist economy. Then it will be possible to develop *The Keynes Solution* for our economic problems—a solution that requires cooperative agreements between government and private enterprise to produce a truly civilized economic society for our children and all future generations.

Chapter 4

A PENNY SPENT IS A PENNY EARNED

Keynes's Ideas on a Capitalist Economy and the Role of Money

In his *General Theory*, John Maynard Keynes stated that classical economists

> resemble Euclidean Geometers in a non Euclidean world who, discovering that in experience straight lines apparently parallel often meet, rebuke the lines for not keeping straight—as the only remedy for the unfortunate collisions which are occurring. Yet in truth there is no remedy except to throw over the axiom of parallels and to work out a non Euclidean geometry. Something similar is required today in economics.[1]

In this analogy, Keynes was alluding to the fact that in the classical analysis, where the future is known, free markets are efficient since they produce full employment (the equivalent of the "parallel lines"). Yet significant and persistent unemployment (the "unfortunate collisions") occur in the real world. Accordingly, classical economists rebuking the lines in the real world for not keeping straight is equivalent to blaming the workers for their unemployment problems because workers would not accept lower wages.

To create a non-Euclidean economics to explain why these unemployment "collisions" occur in the world of experience, Keynes had to deny ("throw over") the relevance of several classical axioms for understanding the real world. The classical ergodic axiom, which assumes that the future is known and can be calculated as the statistical shadow of the past, was one of the most important classical assertions that Keynes rejected.

It should be noted that the famous financial market participant George Soros has explained why the efficient market theory is not applicable to real-world financial markets. In an article entitled "The Crisis and What to Do about It" that appeared in the December 4, 2008, issue of the *New York Review of Books*, Soros wrote that we must abandon the prevailing efficient market theory of market behavior. Instead, he insists that we should recognize that there is a connection between market prices and the underlying reality, a reality that Soros calls reflexivity.

What is this reflexivity? In a letter to the editor published in the March 15–21, 1997, issue of *The Economist*, Soros objects to Paul Samuelson's insistence on applying the ergodic axiom to economics. Soros argues that the Samuelson ergodic hypothesis does not permit "the reflexive interaction between participants' thinking and the actual state of affairs" that characterizes real-world financial markets. In other words, the way people think about the market can affect and alter the future path the market takes. Soros's concept of reflexivity, therefore, is the equivalent of Keynes's throwing over of the ergodic axiom.

In place of the rejected ergodic axiom, Keynes argued that when crucial economic decisions had to be made, decision makers could not merely assume that the future can be reduced to quantifiable risks calculated from already existing market data.

For decisions that involved potential large spending outflows or possible large income inflows that span a significant length of time, people "know" that they do not know what the future will be. They do know that for these important decisions, making a mistake about the future can be very costly; therefore, sometimes putting off a commitment today may be the most judicious decision possible.

Our modern capitalist society has attempted to create an arrangement that will provide people with some control over their uncertain economic destinies. In capitalist economies, the use of money and legally binding money contracts to organize production, sales, and purchases of goods and services permits individuals to have some control over their cash inflows and outflows and therefore some control over their monetary economic future. For example, households enter into contracts where they agree to pay rent or mortgage loan payments on their homes and also contracts to pay electric, gas, and telephone utility companies for providing services over time. These contracts provide the households with some cost control over major aspects of their cost of living today and for months and perhaps years to come. They also provide the other parties (business firms) to these money contracts with the legal promise of current and future cash inflows sufficient to meet their costs of production and generate a profit.

People and business firms willingly enter into contracts because each party thinks it is in its best self-interest to fulfill the terms of the contractual agreement. If, because of some unforeseen event, either party to a contract finds itself unable or unwilling to meet its contractual commitments, then the judicial branch of the government will enforce the contract and require the defaulting party either to meet its contractual obligations or to pay a sum of money sufficient to reimburse the other party for damages and losses incurred. Thus, as Lord Robert Skidelsky, the biographer of Keynes, has noted, for Keynes "injustice is a matter of uncertainty, justice a matter of contractual predictability."[2] In other words, by entering into contractual arrangements, people assure themselves of a measure of predictability in terms of their contractual cash inflows and outflows, even in a world of uncertainty.

Money is that thing that the government has decided will settle all legal contractual obligations. This definition of money is much wider than the definition of legal tender printed on Federal Reserve notes, the paper currency of the United States: "This note is legal tender for all debts, private and public." These notes are liabilities of the Federal Reserve banking system.

For technical reasons regarding the banking system that I need not discuss here, the government permits the use of checks drawn on checking deposit bank accounts as well as the tendering of legal tender currency to discharge any contractual obligations. In fact, readers will recognize that they pay most of their bills (contractual obligations) with checks drawn on their bank accounts, or, in this day of Internet electronic banking, by sending an electronic note to their bank to take a sufficient sum from their account to pay specific billers.

An individual is said to be liquid if he or she can meet all contractual obligations as they come due. For business firms and households, the maintenance of liquid status is of prime importance if bankruptcy is to be avoided. In our world, bankruptcy is the economic equivalent of a walk to the gallows. Maintaining one's liquidity permits a person or business firm to avoid the gallows of bankruptcy.

We all are aware of our own need to maintain liquidity. This need for liquidity typically takes the form of our making sure that we maintain a positive balance in our checkbooks over time so that we can meet all contractual obligations as they come due. If, in any month, we write so many checks that we are close to overdrawing our account, we typically solve this problem in one of three ways:

1. We stop writing any more checks until next month's income is deposited into our account.

2. We arrange for a bank line of credit, where the banker agrees to replenish our bank balance if we should overdraw our account. In return, we typically promise to pay the banker an interest payment and repay the loan principal out of our contractual future cash income.
3. We sell a liquid financial asset in our portfolio and use the money to replenish our bank account.

Obviously a negative checkbook balance is an economic disaster for all members of our capitalist economic system. But why should a person desire to maintain a positive balance rather than a zero balance? Keynes's response would be that since the future is uncertain, we never know when we might be suddenly faced with a payment obligation at a future date that we did not, and could not, anticipate, and which we could not meet out of the cash inflows expected at that future date. Or else we might find that an expected cash inflow suddenly disappears for an unexpected reason—for example, because of a reduction in pension income due to financial market value declines, or a loss of job, or the death of the family's breadwinner.

Accordingly, we have a precautionary liquidity motive for maintaining a positive bank balance in order to protect us from unforeseen events. In a capitalist economy where we know that the future is uncertain, enhancing our liquidity position to cushion the blow of any unanticipated events that may occur is an understandable human activity.

If individuals suddenly believe that the future is more uncertain than it was yesterday, their fear of the future increases. Thus, they will try to reduce cash outflow payments for goods and services today in order to increase their liquidity position so as to be better able to handle any uncertain adverse future events. The most obvious way of reducing cash outflow is to spend less income on produced goods and services—that is, to save more out of current income. If, however, many people suddenly think that the future is more uncertain, then the cumulative effects of all that reduction in spending on the products of industry will result in a significant market decline for the output of business firms. Faced with this decline in market demand, businesses are likely to reduce hiring of workers.

In contrast, if markets in the real world were truly efficient, then households and business firms would have reliable knowledge of the future, including all of their future commitments for contractual cash inflows and cash outflows. Self-interested decision makers, therefore, would never enter into a contract that requires a future payment obligation they could not meet. No one would ever default on a contractual obligation. Consequently, there would never be a need for an additional liquidity cushion to meet an unexpected problem with one's cash flow balances. Yet in the real world, households, business firms, and even local governments do default on contractual obligations.

In fact, the subprime mortgage crisis occurred because there was a significant rate of defaults on mortgages that had been packaged into mortgage-backed securities. (In chapter 6, I explain why the default problems in subprime mortgages created conditions that resulted in the financial crisis that exploded onto the global economy in 2008.)

Since efficient market theory, by assumption, eliminates the possibility of people defaulting on their contractual obligations, it should be obvious that this classical theory cannot logically explain the relationship between the subprime mortgage problem and the global financial crisis that began in 2007. Nor can the efficient market theory provide any guidelines to resolve the global financial crisis except to recommend leaving the problem to the free market to resolve and in the long run allowing the economy to right itself. In chapter 2, I cited Paul Krugman's estimate of the damage done by mortgage defaults where perhaps more than one million people have been, or will be, thrown out of their homes. Those homeowners who remain in their homes will lose $6 trillion of equity value. Can anyone seriously think that such a free market solution is socially desirable or even efficient?

In a Keynesian analysis, however, the civil law of contracts and the importance of maintaining liquidity play crucial roles in understanding the operations of a capitalist economy—both from a domestic national standpoint and in the context of a globalized economy where nations may employ different currencies and even different civil laws of contracts. Chapter 8 covers the international aspect of money and contracts. For now, let me limit the discussion to the implications of domestic money and contracts for the domestic economy.

In Keynes's view, *the sanctity of money contracts is the essence of the entrepreneurial system we call capitalism.* Since money is that thing that can always discharge a contractual obligation under the civil law of contracts, money is the most liquid of all assets. Nevertheless, there exist other liquid assets; their liquidity is somewhat lower than money, since they cannot be "tendered"— handed to the other party in a contract to discharge a contractual obligation. Nevertheless, as long as these other assets can be resold readily for money (liquidated) in a well-organized and orderly financial market, these other assets possess a degree of liquidity. A rapid sale of the asset for money in such a financial market will permit people to use the money received to meet their contractual obligations.

For example, stocks traded on the New York Stock Exchange are not money. Nevertheless, these securities are liquid because the exchange has rules and institutions that are designed to assure people that they can always buy or sell as much stock as they desire while also assuring them that the market price will always change in an orderly manner. By "orderly manner," I mean that the price on the next sale of a stock transaction to be executed will not differ by very much from the price of the previous transaction. Thus, when a person calls his broker and tells the broker to sell x shares "at the market," the seller knows that the price to be received will not differ by more than a few pennies from the last announced market transaction price.

As Peter L. Bernstein, author of the bestseller *Against the Gods*, has noted, the existence of orderly financial markets for liquid assets encourages all holders (investors) of these securities to believe they can execute a fast exit strategy at any moment when they suddenly decide they are dissatisfied with the way things are happening. Without liquidity for these stocks, the risks of being a minority stockholder (owner) in a business enterprise would be intolerable. Nevertheless, the liquidity of orderly equity markets and markets' encouragement of fast exit strategies make the separation of ownership and control (management) of business enterprises an important problem that economists and politicians have puzzled over since the 1930s. The surprise that many experts have expressed that the *managers* of large investment bankers were not protecting the interests of the *owners* of these corporations indicates that they do not understand how the existence of orderly liquid markets drives an important wedge between ownership and management. Classical efficient market theory implicitly assumes that those who own the firm will either manage the firm directly or hire managers (workers) who, if they want to stay employed, will pursue the same self-interested objectives that the owners would pursue if the latter actively managed the firm. In other words, in classical theory, there can never be a decision-making separation between owners and managers.

If I am a minority stockholder (and most stockholders are) of any large public corporation and I do not like the way management has been operating, I will immediately sell my shares rather than engage in a costly and lengthy process of attempting to fire the managers who, in my opinion, have made bad mistakes in the operation of the corporation.

In chapter 6, I explain why, as long as the future is uncertain, the price that liquid assets can sell for at any future date in a free market can vary dramatically and almost instantaneously. In the worst-case scenario, financial assets can become unsalable (illiquid) at any price as the market for that asset collapses (fails) in a disorderly manner.

To assure holders of liquid securities that the market price for their holdings will *always change in an orderly manner*, there must exist in the marketplace a person or firm called a "market maker." The existence of this market maker assures the public that if, at any time, many holders of the financial asset suddenly want to execute a fast exit strategy and sell, while few or no people want to buy this liquid asset, the market maker will be obligated to enter the market and purchase a sufficient volume of the asset to ensure that the following market transaction prices of the asset will change continuously in an "orderly" manner from the price of the last transaction. In essence, the market maker assures holders of liquid assets that they can always execute a fast exit strategy at a price not much different from the last price. In the New York Stock Exchange, these market makers are called "specialists."

A Penny Saved Is a Penny Not Earned

In a money-using, capitalist system where people recognize that the future is uncertain, households and business firms will want to maintain a liquid position. To obtain a significant liquid position, therefore, typically people will try not to spend all of their cash inflows (money incomes) on the products of industry each week, month, or year. We call this unspent portion of money income "savings." To carry these savings—that is, contractual settlement power—into the future, savers use a variety of liquid "time machines": money under the mattress, positive balances in the savers' bank accounts, buying and holding in a portfolio a variety of financial assets such as stocks, bonds, or other financial assets that savers believe have a high degree of liquidity due to the fact that they are being traded in a well-organized and orderly market. Unfortunately, as I explain in chapter 6, the market has become disorderly for financial assets known as CDOs (collateralized debt obligations) and other exotic financial derivatives. The result was the financial market crisis that began in 2007.

At this point, it is important to note that any portion of one's income that is not spent on the products of industry must mean a lesser demand for those products of industry than what the demand would be if all the income was spent. Thus, savings can have a negative impact on business profits and employment hiring by firms.[3]

What creates jobs in a capitalist economy? Although government creates some jobs and hires workers—members of police and fire departments, the armed forces, teachers in public schools and public universities, judges, and the like—the majority of jobs are created in the private sector by business firms hiring workers. Recessions and depressions occur when firms are laying off large numbers of workers; prosperity occurs when firms are making good profits and hiring almost everyone who is willing and able to work.

What determines whether firms hire or fire workers? Expectation of increasing sales provides the positive incentives for business firms to hire more workers to produce additional output to sell at a profitable price. If, however, business firms expect (or experience) declining sales that imply declining profit opportunities, firms will reduce the number of employees they hire or employ. In sum, changes in expected future sales and orders will have a dominant effect on the hiring practices of private sector employers.

Consequently, anything that causes a decline in total spending on the goods and services produced by a country's business firms tends to depress employment; anything that increases spending on goods and services increases the profitability of business firms and the hiring of workers. Thus, contrary to Benjamin Franklin's saying that "a penny saved is a penny earned," it is only every penny that is spent on the products of industry that becomes a penny earned to be shared by workers, managers, and business owners.

An act of saving out of current income means that the purchases on the output of industry will be less than if the entire income was spent and nothing was saved. A penny saved cannot be earned by business firms selling goods and services. Savings represent less profit opportunities for business to make a sale, and therefore firms will hire fewer workers than otherwise. It therefore follows that if, in total, all buyers of products and services decide to spend less and instead increase their savings, then less profitable market demand will be available to businesses, and firms will offer less employment.

Of course, the job-destroying potential of some savers can be offset if, at the same time, other buyers decide to spend more than before and even to go into debt to increase their purchases of goods and services from business enterprises.

Who are these other buyers, and why will they be willing to go into debt to spend more?

Economists tend to identify four classes of buyers of goods and services produced by business firms: (1) households; (2) business firms investing in additional plant and equipment because they anticipate future sales to exceed their current capacity to produce; (3) government, including state and local governments as well as the federal government; and (4) foreigners who want to buy our exports.

I discuss the effect of export sales in chapter 7 when I deal with the question of foreign trade. So, at this stage, let us concentrate on the first three categories of buyers.

Household purchases tend to be tied closely to income. If household income increases, households tend to increase their purchases of goods and services, and if their income declines, they tend to spend less. If the economy is in a recession or depression, it is because some buyers of the products of private enterprise are, for whatever reason, buying less and fewer workers are being employed. Thus, a recession is always associated with a decline in the total of all household income as some workers are fired and have to live on lower unemployment compensation, while other households that obtain part of their income from the profit of firms find these sums reduced as business firms experience lower sales receipts.

What about investment spending by firms? Classical theory asserts that if markets are efficient, whenever households save more, simultaneously business firms will borrow these savings and spend more investing in plant and equipment. Does anyone really believe that if people are saving more and buying less from business firms, business firms, in face of this decline in market demand, immediately invest more in additional capacity to enable them to produce more product?

If market demand is declining and firms are feeling the effects of recession, managers are unlikely to purchase new plant and equipment when they already have capacity that has been idled by this decline in sales and orders. Even if interest rates are reduced significantly to make it inexpensive to borrow to buy new plant and equipment from firms that produce these capital goods, managers are unlikely to borrow. Business firms will start reinvesting in plant and equipment only after market demand has risen sufficiently so that firms believe that sales will be pressing on existing capacity. Accordingly, in a recession, we cannot expect enterprises to increase their spending on investment.

Consequently, government is the only possible big spender to offset falling sales and profits. Unfortunately, most state and local government spending is tied closely to the tax revenue base, and in a recession, governments quickly experience a shortfall in their expected tax receipts compared to their existing budget. In many states and municipalities, the revenue decline means an immediate reduction in the provision of public services and the firing of government workers, which only swells the ranks of the unemployed and reduces market demand for the products of industry even more.

In the current recession, one of the cuts state and local governments are making is to public colleges and universities, community colleges, and public schools. The result is not only an increase in unemployment of highly skilled and educated workers, but also a reduction in the quality of public education at all levels, thereby robbing our children of the opportunity to obtain a quality education. Local governments will also cut back or suspend investments in the infrastructure that makes living in a community satisfying.

Accordingly, in a recession, it is just the federal government that is able not only to maintain but actually to increase spending on the products of private enterprise, even if its tax receipts are due to declining incomes for business firms and households. Of course, to buy more while revenues are declining, the federal government must finance these purchases by borrowing money—that is, by increasing the annual deficit and adding to the national debt, which at the end of 2008 already totaled $10 trillion.

The Keynes Solution for recession and depression is to develop a recovery spending plan that may require significant to massive government expenditures. But these massive expenditures are not at all bad. Remember, if this spending is used to buy the products of the nation's business firms, the result will be to create massive profit opportunities for American business firms, which, in turn, will create a significant increase in the number of job hires in the private sector, restoring prosperity to American households.

What Should the Government Buy?

When significant unemployment and idle capacity exist, increased government expenditures will swell market demand, creating profit opportunities for firms to expand output and hire more workers. Depending on what government buys from private enterprise, specific industries will have the incentive to expand output and employment.

Consequently, what things should government purchase? Obviously, government purchases that improve its citizens' productivity and lives will be very desirable. Thus, President Obama has suggested an economic recovery plan that contracts with business firms to restore and improve the infrastructure that serves communities around the nation. The Obama plan would include spending funds to encourage private enterprise to develop alternative sources of energy, such as solar panels, windmills, hybrid energy-efficient automobiles, and the like.

Yet many in politics object to spending significant sums on such projects. Often these same people who object to spending large sums on things that can be useful to the civilian population would not hesitate to spend similar sums to purchase from industry all sorts of military equipment. This policy of spending on military equipment is often referred to as military Keynesianism. Until now, it has been the main form of Keynes's spending policy that has been acceptable to conservative politicians.

Nevertheless, ideological free market advocates tend to oppose a strong government spending recovery program. Typically they raise three basic objections to any large-scale budget recovery program:

1. If we increase the national debt, we will cause the nation to go bankrupt. Proponents of this argument typically compare the government to a household. We all understand that households that run up too much debt relative to their income ultimately face bankruptcy. If households cannot deficit spend indefinitely, why should our government be able to?

2. If we increase the national debt, we will burden our children and our grandchildren with paying off this debt, and they will suffer for our profligacy.

3. Government spending will be financed by the government "printing money." This increase in the total money supply will create—if not immediately, then at some time in the foreseeable (certain?) future—a Great Inflation.

In the next chapter I explain the fallacies in these three arguments. With the U.S. economy in a deep recession in 2009 and the global economy falling into the same hole, the question should not be whether we can afford a deficit spending recovery program to restore profits, jobs, and prosperity to the U.S. economy. The real question should be: Can we afford *not* to deficit spend enough to restore prosperity to the U.S. economy? If we do not pursue an active government spending recovery plan, our children and grandchildren will face a dismal economic future with little prospect of jobs and decent incomes over most of their lives, even if they inherit a government with a smaller total national debt.

This generation owes it to future generations to actively build a persistently prosperous capitalist system where profit opportunities are readily available and where all who want to work and earn a decent standard of living are given the opportunity to do so.

Chapter 5

THE TRUTH ABOUT THE NATIONAL DEBT AND INFLATION

When President George W. Bush left office on January 20, 2009, the United States government debt was $9.2 trillion, an amount equal to almost 70 percent of the gross domestic product (GDP). Some have expressed a fear that the nation will go bankrupt if the government continues to spend in excess of tax receipts.

Is the National Debt Too Large?

As early as 1790, the newly formed United States of America already had a national debt of approximately $75 million as the government assumed the debts that had been incurred during the Revolutionary War. Except for a short period during the 1830s when the federal government's debt was reduced to zero, the U.S. government has always had some outstanding debt. During World

War I, the national debt increased substantially, from $1.2 billion in 1916 to $25.4 billion in 1919.

The prosperous decade of the Roaring Twenties saw a decline in the national debt. By 1929, the total debt had been reduced to $16.9 billion, or approximately 16 percent of GDP. This reduction in the debt was a result of the federal government spending $5.8 billion less than its tax revenue receipts between 1919 and 1929. In other words, through most of the decade of the 1920s, the federal government savings were substantial. Yet the economy continued to grow and prosper. This experience indicates that if and when the private sector is spending sufficiently to buy most of the products that industry can produce, there is no need for the government to deficit spend merely to maintain a prosperous economy.

Beginning in 1929, however, total private spending suddenly declined, and the Great Depression began. As sales of goods and services collapsed, business profits were devastated, and unemployment rose rapidly. Household incomes declined. As a result, tax revenues declined from $4 billion in 1930 to less than $2 billion in 1932. When Franklin Roosevelt took office in March 1933, the national debt had increased to almost $20 billion, a sum equal to 20 percent of the GDP of the United States at the time.

As noted in chapter 2, the Roosevelt administration ran large annual deficits during its first term. By 1936, the national debt had increased to $33.7 billion, or approximately 40 percent of GDP. Many experts of that era said disaster awaited the nation if it continued to deficit spend. Accordingly, Roosevelt cut government spending in fiscal year 1937—and the economy immediately fell into a steep recession. The government resumed significant deficit spending in 1938. By 1940, the economy had grown substantially while the national debt rose to $43 billion—approximately 44 percent of GDP.

When the United States entered World War II in 1941, the fear of deficits and the size of the national debt were forgotten. In the years from 1941 to 1945, the GDP more than doubled while the national debt increased by more than 500 percent. By the end of 1945, the national debt was equal to approximately 119 percent of GDP. Rather than bankrupting the nation when the war ended, this large national debt promoted a prosperous economy. By 1946, the average American household was living much better economically than in the prewar days. Moreover, the children and grandchildren of the Great Depression–World War II generation have not been burdened by having to pay off what was then considered a huge national debt. Instead, for the next quarter of a century, the economy continued on a path of unprecedented economic growth and prosperity. At the same time, the inequality in the distribution of income was significantly narrowed. It was the golden age of economic development for the United States.

As a child of the depression and a young teenager during World War II, I have never felt burdened by those huge government deficits. The great generation who were adults during those years left to their children a legacy of abundance and prosperity. I inherited an economy that made finding a good job easy for me and my cohorts and provided excellent opportunities to improve our living standard. If this is burdening children and grandchildren, I hope the current generation can create such a "burden" for their progeny.

The moral of this story is that we have nothing to fear about running big government deficits when government is the only spender that can increase market demand for the products of our industries and thereby maintain a profitable entrepreneurial system. For government to spend less in the hopes of keeping down the size of the national debt would mean causing market demand to remain slack and thereby impoverishing both our business firms and our workers.

Keynes's idea was that capitalism works best when spenders cause healthy growth in market demands and thereby generate profits and jobs for the community. This was clearly demonstrated when government spending increased during the years 1933 to 1936 and 1938 to 1945. When Roosevelt cut spending in fiscal year 1937, the resulting sharp recession showed that at that stage of recovery, no other spenders were willing or able to take over the role of market demand generator. Had Roosevelt, in 1938, continued on the path of keeping government spending in check in order not to increase the total national debt, he would have propagated a poorly performing economy. When the war broke out and no further thought was given to the size of the national debt, government spending quickly pushed the economy to a profitable full-employment status. This historical record validates Keynes's ideas about the operation of a capitalist economy.

Will Printing Money Create a "Great Inflation"?

In order to rescue the economy from a serious recession, government should undertake significant additional spending and therefore incur deficits that are in whole or part financed by selling bonds to the Federal Reserve. In essence, this means that the deficit is financed by "printing money."

Won't this increase in the money supply create a great inflation? For example, in the January 29, 2009, issue of the *Wall Street Journal*, in an article entitled "Fed Inches toward Plan to Purchase U.S. Bonds," reporters J. Hilsenrath and L. Rappaport wrote about the Fed's plan to purchase government bonds: "[I]t would be a controversial move at a time when government budget deficits are soaring. Some might see it as an inflationary move to finance deficits by printing money."

There is, of course, this old wives' tale—propagated even by Nobel Prize economists such as Milton Friedman—that when the money supply increases as government "prints" money to spend, rapid inflation is inevitable.

How does this printing money process actually work? To the extent that the government wants to spend more than it takes in in tax revenue, the government must sell bonds. If the government cannot find any savers in the private sector of the economy to buy these bonds, it can sell the bonds to the Federal Reserve. In essence, the Fed purchases these government debt instruments by giving the United States Treasury a credit on the Treasury's account at the Fed. The Treasury can then write checks against this increase in its account at the Fed. Since checks drawn on legitimate bank accounts can settle contractual obligations, the increase in the Treasury's account is the equivalent of the government printing money. But if the government spending of this money goes to encouraging firms to increase output and employment, why should it create inflation?

This idea of a direct connection between deficit spending financed by printing money and inflation is a logical deduction that follows from a fundamental second axiom that is the basis of mainstream classical efficient market models, the *neutral money axiom*.

This neutral money axiom asserts that any increases in the supply of money into the economy will affect neither the volume of goods produced nor the level of employment in the economy. In other words, the neutral money axiom asserts *as a universal truth that does not have to be proven* that any increases in the quantity of money supplied will have absolutely no effect on the amount of goods and services produced (GDP) or on the level of employment.

It follows that if the neutral money presumption is built into the economic model, then if the government "prints" money to spend on the products of industry, inflation is inevitable. If the government spends all these "printed" additional dollars, the result must be an increase in the market demand for goods and services. If you accept the neutral money axiom, however, the increased market demand created by the government printing money cannot affect the total amount of goods and services that entrepreneurs will produce and sell in the market. The neutral money assumption means that this increase in market demand cannot encourage entrepreneurs to expand output and hire more workers. This increase in market demand can only raise market prices and therefore cause inflation. Hence classical economists are merely assuming that deficit spending financed by printing money causes inflation since "too much money is chasing too few goods." These classical economists have not proven, and believe that they need not prove, that printing money causes inflation. Since the neutral money axiom is a fundamental building block of efficient market theory, classical economists merely assert that inflation occurs when the supply of money increases faster than output.

Blind acceptance of the neutral money assumption prevents a logically consistent analyst from recognizing that if there is significant unemployment and idle capacity, then the additional government deficit spending can and will create profit opportunities and therefore induce business firms to expand output and employment. In this case, the increase in the money supply "printed" to finance additional government spending need not cause inflation.

When things get tough, even the people who accept mainstream economic theory with its fundamental neutral money assumption may recognize that this theory is not applicable. The aforementioned *Wall Street Journal* article goes on to state: "With economic slack building so abruptly around the world, Fed officials don't see inflation as a worry now." But if not now, would inflation from printing money ever occur when the economy recovers and there are more goods and services produced for sale, with this same quantity of money already existing? Won't we have the same quantity of money chasing far more goods?

It may be a surprise to learn that advocates admit that the neutral money assumption is an article of faith, not fact. Referring to economic models used by prestigious economic institutions to predict the future of the economy, Professor Oliver Blanchard of the Massachusetts Institute of Technology and chief economist for the International Monetary Fund has stated: "All the models we have seen impose the neutrality of money as a maintained assumption. This is very much a matter of faith based on theoretical considerations rather than empirical evidence."[1]

Keynes, however, argued that one had to throw over the classical neutral money axiom as well as the ergodic axiom in order to explain the operations of a capitalist system in our world of experience. While Keynes was still working out his revolutionary analysis in 1933, he wrote:

> The theory which I desiderate would deal…with an economy in which money plays a part of its own and affects motives and decisions and is, in short, one of the operative factors in the situation, so that the course of events cannot be predicted either in the long period or in the short, without a knowledge of the behaviour of money between the first state and the last. And it is this which we ought to mean when we speak of *a monetary economy.*…Booms and depressions are peculiar to an economy in which…*money is not neutral.*[2]

In removing the neutral money axiom from his analytical framework, Keynes was denying that barter transactions—where goods trade for goods—are the essence of our economic system. Money plays an important role in the operation of a capitalist economy. In his analysis, additional spending financed by increasing the money supply was more likely to induce entrepreneurs to produce more product to sell and earn additional profits. In the absence of a neutral money axiom, it is possible that financing additional spending via increasing the money supply will not be inflationary whenever significant unemployment and idle capacity exist.

Explaining Inflation

Inflation occurs whenever there is a significant increase in the money prices of most goods and services that residents of a nation purchase. If the neutrality of money axiom is rejected as merely an article of faith, as Blanchard readily admits, then we should not have a knee-jerk reaction that says that when the government prints money and spends on a recovery plan, it must be inflationary.

Then what causes inflation? In a two-volume work entitled *A Treatise on Money*, published in 1930, Keynes identified two different types of inflation, commodity inflation and incomes inflation. Although each type of inflation was associated with a rising price level, each type had a different cause.

Commodity Inflation

Commodity inflation is identified essentially with rising market prices of durable standardized commodities, such as agricultural products, crude oil, and minerals. These commodities typically are traded on well-organized public markets, and the market prices are reported in newspapers and other media. These markets tend to have prices associated with a specific date of delivery—either delivery today or at a specific date in the future.

Many commodity markets for future deliveries are limited to dates in only a few months—typically no more than ten months or less. Since most commodities take a significant length of time to produce, their supply for any near-future date in these markets is assumed to be relatively fixed by already existing stocks plus any semifinished products currently in the pipeline and expected to be finished by the near-future date of delivery. If there is a sudden increase in demand for delivery in the near future in these public markets and it is expected that little or no augmentation to the existing supply is available on that market date, this increase in market demand will only inflate the market's future price of these commodities. Similarly, if there is any sudden change in available supply, with no change in market demand, market prices will change. For example, say a sudden frost destroys crops in the ground that are almost ready to be harvested. Given no change in demand, we should expect crop commodity prices to rise, causing a commodity inflation.

We are all familiar with stories about commodity speculators who buy up significant inventories and withhold these inventories from the market (reducing available supply) in order to inflate the commodity market price. If these speculators are successful, they can later sell their inventory at a profit. Such successful speculators are said to have "cornered the market" and have contributed to a commodity inflation.

Since a commodity price inflation occurs whenever there is a sudden and unforeseen change in demand or available supply for delivery in the near future, this type of inflation can be avoided easily by an institution that is not motivated by self-interest but instead wants to protect society from inflationary pressures. Preventing commodity price inflation requires the government to maintain an inventory of the commodity as a buffer stock to prevent changes in demand and/or supply from inducing significant price movements. A buffer stock is nothing more than some commodity shelf inventory that can be moved into and out of the market to buffer the market from disorderly price disruptions by offsetting previously unforeseen changes in demand or supply as they occur.

For example, since the oil price shocks of the 1970s, the United States has developed a strategic petroleum reserve where crude oil is stored in underground salt domes on the coast of the Gulf of Mexico. These oil reserves are designed to provide emergency market supplies to buffer the market price of domestic oil if there is a sudden decrease in supplies from the politically unstable Middle East. The strategic use of such a petroleum reserve means that the price of oil will not increase as much as it otherwise would if, for example, a political crisis broke out in the Middle East.

In other words, an oil price inflation could be avoided as long as the buffer stock remains available to offset any immediately available commodity shortage. Thus, during the short Desert

Storm war against Iraq in 1991, U.S. government officials made oil from the strategic petroleum reserves available to the market to offset the possibility of disruptions (actual or expected) affecting the market price of crude oil. The Department of Energy estimated that this use of a buffer stock prevented the price of gasoline at the pump from rising about 30 cents per gallon.

Use of buffer stocks as a public policy solution to commodity price inflation is as old as the biblical story of Joseph and the Pharaoh's dream of seven fat cows followed by seven lean cows. Joseph—the economic forecaster of his day—interpreted the Pharaoh's dream as portending seven good harvests where production (supply) would be much above normal, causing prices (and farmers' incomes) to be below normal. Seven lean harvests would follow; annual production would not provide enough food to go around while prices farmers received would be exorbitantly high. Joseph's civilized anti-inflation policy proposal was for the government to store up a buffer stock of grain during the good years and to release the grain to market, without profit, during the bad years. This would maintain a stable price over the 14 harvests, avoid inflation in the bad years, and protect farmers' incomes in the good harvest years. According to the Bible, this civilized buffer stock policy was a resounding economic success.

The inflation in oil and some agricultural commodities that exploded in the summer of 2008 was based on the (false) expectation that with China and India growing so rapidly, their increased demand for these commodities, when added to normal demand from other nations, would quickly push up the market price to astronomical levels. Some experts predicted that crude oil would hit $200 a barrel by the beginning of 2009. If these expectations were rational, then speculators could buy oil in the market for, say, $100 per barrel and then turn around and in a short time resell it, making 100 percent profit.

Accordingly, not only speculators, but also large users of petroleum products, such as the airlines, bought crude oil futures in the marketplace. The airlines bought oil futures in order to assure themselves of a lower price for fuel when by the end of 2008 the price was expected to be $200 a barrel. Of course, when the price of crude oil fell to less than $40 a barrel by the end of 2008, the airlines lost a great deal of money on their purchases, which were based on a speculative belief that crude oil prices would inevitably rise rapidly in 2008 and beyond.

While the commodity inflation was peaking, I published an article in the July/August 2008 issue of *Challenge* magazine, explaining that excessive and unrealistic speculation on the future price of crude oil was leading to a commodity inflation in crude oil prices as well as in agricultural commodities. My argument was based on my knowledge of Keynes's commodity inflation concept and of the operations of the petroleum industry. I had acquired the latter knowledge when I was an assistant director of the economics division of an important oil company and later when I was an expert witness in an antitrust case involving 13 major oil firms. I recognized that a simple policy would stop this speculation in its tracks and result in a significant decline in crude oil prices.

I suggested that the federal government follow the biblical example of Joseph. As prices were nearing $140 a barrel, I wrote that if the government would sell in the market less than 10 percent of the oil that it had accumulated in the strategic petroleum reserve, crude oil prices would fall to less than $100 a barrel. The result not only would reduce the price of petroleum products to consumers but also would turn a profit for the government, as it had bought the oil stored in the strategic petroleum reserve at a much lower price than the current market price.

Although the government did not adopt this buffer stock policy, the financial crisis of 2008 with its recessionary impact deflated this commodity speculation.

If political problems in the Middle East break out during the Obama presidency, I hope that the president will use the buffer stock analogy to stop any oil price inflation that may occur.

Incomes Inflation

Keynes also identified a second form of inflation, incomes inflation, which is associated with the rise in the money costs of production per unit of goods produced. As the costs of production rise, business firms will be forced to raise the market price of their products if they are going to continue to make a profit on what they produce.

These increased money costs of production reflect increased income payments to owners of inputs in the production process: wage and salary earners, material suppliers, lenders, and/or profit recipients. Thus, for example, if the money wage rate increases while worker productivity is unchanged, the labor costs of each unit of output rises. This rise in the unit cost of production requires business firms to raise prices accordingly in order to produce and still make a profit.

In other words, incomes inflation occurs when the money costs of production increase because owners of the inputs to the production process receive higher money incomes that are not offset by productivity increases.

This incomes inflation highlights the obvious but often ignored fact that, given productivity relations, inflationary increases in the prices of domestic producible goods are always associated with (and the result of) an increase in someone's money income earned in the production process. A firm's costs of production are the other side of the coin of the income of people who provide labor, materials, property, or capital for use by the firm in the production process.

If the government is to constrain the rate of incomes inflation of domestically producible goods and services, it must somehow constrain the rise in the money income of inputs in the production process to improvements in productivity. Rises in money wages, salaries, and other material costs in production contracts always imply increases in someone's money income.

With slavery illegal in civilized societies, the money-wage contract for hiring labor is the most universal of all production costs.

Labor costs accounts for the vast majority of production contract costs in the economy, even for such high-technology products as NASA spacecraft. That is why, especially in the 25 years following World War II, inflation typically was associated with money-wage inflation.

Wage contracts typically specify a certain money wage per unit of time. This labor cost plus a profit margin or markup to cover material costs, overhead, and profit on the investment become the basis for managerial decisions as to the prices that must be received to make the undertaking of production profitable. If money wages rise relative to labor productivity, the labor costs of producing output increase. Consequently firms must raise their sales price if they are to maintain profitability and viability. When production costs and therefore contract prices for orders are rising throughout the economy, we are suffering an incomes inflation.

Clearly, to prevent incomes inflation, there must be some constraint on the rate of increase of money incomes relative to productivity. Currently, with the economy falling deeper into recession, most workers, landlords, lenders, and business firms have little power to raise their prices and thus create an incomes inflation atmosphere. Thus, there is little or no threat that the Obama stimulus plan will create an atmosphere that will promote incomes inflation. If, and when, the Obama recovery program lifts the U.S. economy completely out of recession and back toward full-employment prosperity, government will have to be vigilant that it does not create a situation where productive inputs can demand incomes-inflationary price increases. If these incomes-inflationary pressures should arise in the future, what would the Keynes solution be?

Incomes Policy to Fight Incomes Inflation

For many years following World War II, rising money wage rates in most developed nations were a major factor in producing incomes inflation. To understand why this wage-price inflation was particularly rampant, we must recognize the change in the nature of the industrial society that followed the war. As the economist John Kenneth Galbraith noted: "The market with its maturing of industrial society and its associated political institutions...loses radically its authority as a regulatory force...[and] partly it is an expression of our democratic ethos."[3]

After the devastating experiences of the Great Depression, the emerging ethos of the common man in democratic nations held that people should have more control of their economic destiny. The Great Depression had taught everyone that individuals cannot have control of their economic lives if they leave the determination of their income completely to the tyranny of the free market. Consequently, after World War II, in societies with any democratic tendencies, people not only demanded economic security from the capitalist system but also demanded that they play a controlling role in determining their economic destiny. This controlling role required power to control one's income. The result was an institutional power struggle for higher incomes among unions, political coalitions, economic cartels, and monopolistic industries that led to an incomes inflation.

As long as the government guarantees that it will pursue a full-employment policy, all self-interested workers, unions, and business managers have little to fear that their demand for higher prices and money income will result in lost sales and unemployment. As long as the government accepts responsibility for creating sufficient aggregate effective demand to maintain the economy close to a full-employment level of output, there will be no market incentive to stop this recurring struggle over the distribution of income that results in incomes inflation.

Full-employment policies without some deliberate announced incomes constraint policy ensure that there will no longer exist what Karl Marx derogatorily called "the industrial reserve army" of the unemployed who would be willing to obtain employment by accepting a lower wage than those who currently are employed accept. As long as there is a large number of unemployed people, firms are able to resist workers' demands for higher wages. The existence of a large number of unemployed people with similar skills makes employed workers thankful that they still have a job and can earn income. Employed workers, therefore, are less likely to be truculent and demand higher pay in the face of recession and high levels of unemployed workers. In a laissez-faire market environment, a significant percentage of unemployed workers can be a major force to constrain organized workers' demand for higher money wages.

Since the 1990s, with globalized free trade, the almost unlimited supply of unskilled and semiskilled workers in China, India, and elsewhere who are willing to work at much lower wages than those that prevail in the West have acted like Marx's "industrialized army of the unemployed" in limiting the ability of Western workers to increase or even maintain the existing money-wage rate paid for most blue-collar and even some white-collar jobs. The resulting outsourcing of high-paying American jobs to these low-wage countries not only has reduced domestic union power to raise workers' wages and fringe benefits but also has resulted in the destruction or hollowing out of the manufacturing base in the United States. I discuss the problems and policies for dealing with outsourcing and international trade in chapter 7.

According to classical economists who believe in the beneficence of the "invisible hand" of free markets, in the absence of a threat of losing one's job to unemployed workers domestically or to foreigners through outsourcing, there is only one way to combat a wage-incomes inflation. In a free society where people are motivated solely by self-interest, workers and entrepreneurs are free to demand any price for their services, even if such demands are inflationary. The classical solution to incomes inflation is to depress the economy. Accordingly, classical theory implies that one of the rights of a free society is the right to price oneself out of the market.

Of course, if governments guarantee that they will always pursue a full-employment economy, then conceivably one can never price oneself out of the market. In a free market economy where government does not intervene and does not guarantee full employment, there is one obvious way to ensure that inflationary income demands of workers and entrepreneurs will always price them out of the market. When threats of inflationary income demands increase, the nation's central bank can raise interest rates and thereby choke off borrowing and spending in the private sector. The result of this tight money policy will be that profit opportunities will decline and employers will have to fire workers. With increasing unemployment, market demand for the products of industry will decline, and business firms will be very wary of raising wages and/or prices. In other words, in the incomes policy supported by free market advocates, the central bank undertakes a monetary policy to deliberately reduce aggregate spending and market demand.

For example, say a central bank announces that it has a target rate of inflation of 2 percent. This target is set to warn the public that if the measured inflation rate exceeds 2 percent, the central bank will deliberately create a recessionary environment, threatening people's jobs, in order to force people to reduce their inflationary income demands.

In other words, if forces creating a push for rising money income causes prices to rise by more than the target rate, the central bank will raise interest rates until the rate of inflation is again reduced to the target rate, even if this causes widespread unemployment and business losses. Accordingly, a central bank uses an announced target rate of inflation as an instrument to invoke fear in firms and workers: that if they permit (demand) wages and prices to rise, they are in danger of losing the opportunity of earning a living. This policy to constrain demands for money income increases can be called an "incomes policy of fear." The object is to convince the working public that the central bank will stop at nothing to prevent any significant inflationary wage or other income demands from being validated in the marketplace. A tight monetary policy that reduces market demands sufficiently so that the fear of loss of profits strengthens managers' backbone sufficiently to deny workers' wage demands and the fear of unemployment quells workers' demands for improvements in wages and fringe benefits is the anti-incomes inflation policy of classical theory.

If an independent central bank adamantly attacks incomes inflation by creating recessionary forces, classical theorists believe that the resultant slack demand in the marketplace for domestic goods will discipline all workers and firms with the fear of loss of sales and income. Nothing closely approaching full-employment prosperity can be tolerated as long as we rely on the free market's incomes policy of threatening unemployment and enterprise failure. Thus, those who advocate "inflation-targeting" monetary policy by the central bank are implicitly endorsing an incomes policy based on fear: of loss of jobs, sales revenues, and profits for firms that produce goods and services domestically. Fear, it is believed, will keep owners of the domestic factors of production in their place. The amount of slack demand necessary to enforce this incomes policy of fear depends on what some modern classical economists call the domestic "natural rate" of unemployment.

Proponents of this inflation-targeting incomes policy of fear implicitly suggest that the natural unemployment rate will be smaller if government "liberalizes" labor markets by reducing, if not completely eliminating, long-term unemployment benefits or other money income supports, including minimum wages, employer contributions to pension funds, health insurance for employees, legislation protecting working conditions, and union organizing of workers. Then workers will be less truculent.

Free market advocates often view a permanent social safety net to protect the unemployed as mollycoddling casualties in the war against inflation so that others may think there is little to fear if they join the ranks of the unemployed. A ubiquitous and overwhelming fear instilled in all members of society is a necessary condition for the barbarous inflation-targeting program to work. Inevitably, civil society is the first casualty of this war.

In essence, this free market view for fighting inflation has not progressed very far from the advice that Secretary Mellon gave President Hoover: "Liquidate labor....It will purge the rottenness out of the system. People will work harder, lead a more moral life."[4]

With the integration of populous nations such as China and India into the global economy of the twenty-first century, another "industrial reserve army" has been introduced into the economies of many developed nations. The promotion of "free trade" has begun to instill fear in high-wage domestic workers who might lose their jobs to foreign low-wage workers. These low-wage populous nations have an almost unlimited supply of idle and unemployed workers who are willing to accept jobs at wages much below those prevailing in the major developed nations. This fact combined with the growing phenomenon of outsourcing of manufacturing jobs and services incomes (where a service is produced, e.g., a call center in India, transportation and communication costs are relatively small) has resulted in significantly humbling and constraining income demands of the labor forces of major industrial nations in the last two decades. As a result, incomes inflation has been limited to those domestic service occupations and manufacturing industries (e.g., national defense) where outsourcing is not an alternative. Thus, there has been a growing inequality of income between the unskilled and semiskilled workers in Western industrial nations and the Western managers and owners of multinational corporations who can outsource their lower-end jobs while demanding higher profit margins and executive salaries and bonuses on sales of their products.

For those who find the classical theory's anti–incomes inflation policy not a very civilized action against fellow citizens, an alternative anti-inflation incomes policy can be developed from Keynes's ideas regarding inflation.

In 1970, before outsourcing became a major weapon to keep labor in its place, Professor Sidney Weintraub of the University of Pennsylvania recognized the relevance of Keynes's incomes inflation concept to the bouts of inflation nations were suffering prior to the oil price shock of 1973. Weintraub then developed a "clever" anti-inflation policy called TIP—a tax-based incomes policy. TIP required the use of the corporate income tax structure to penalize the largest domestic firms in the economy if they agreed to wage rate increases in excess of some national productivity improvement standard. Thus, the tax system would be used to penalize those firms that agreed to inflationary wage demands. The hope of TIP was that if wage increases could be limited to overall productivity increases, then workers and owners of all other inputs to the domestic production process would willingly accept noninflationary monetary income increases.

Weintraub believed two conditions were necessary if TIP was to be an effective policy that did not rely on "fear" of loss of income to constrain incomes inflation. These conditions are:

1. TIP was to be a permanent policy institution.
2. TIP must be a penalty system, not a reward (subsidy) tax system.

Once instituted, TIP could never be removed; otherwise, as it reached its termination date, it would lose its effectiveness. Weintraub stated that the magnitude of tax penalties could be altered as conditions warranted but a threat of penalties must always exist to ensure compliance.

A reward TIP—one that reduced people's taxes if they adhered to the national wage standard—would be administratively unworkable, as everyone would claim the reward and the government would have to prove which claimants were not entitled to the reduction in taxes. According to Weintraub, TIP was similar to the way government enforces speed limits on the nation's highways. If you exceed the speed limit—which is always in place—you pay a speeding fine. Governments never pay good drivers for not exceeding the speed limit.

Unfortunately, the United States and many other nations have never seriously attempted to develop a permanent penalty-oriented TIP. Instead, under the banner of free trade, outsourcing has been our incomes policy. Multinational firms with ready access to unlimited supplies of low-paid workers in less developed nations have held down wage demands.

The real cost of such an incomes policy to many industrialized nations in the recent past has been significant. For Germany and France, for instance, double-digit unemployment rates—previously unseen since the Great Depression—often are the norm.

Weintraub, the perpetual believer in the use of human intelligence rather than brute (market) forces to encourage socially compatible civilized behavior, believed that, ultimately, some form of civilized incomes constraint policy would be seen as a more humane way to control inflation without the necessary depressing side effects of traditional classical inflation-targeting policy. Weintraub believed it was possible to pursue a full-employment economic policy, as long as a civilized society installed an incomes policy that treated all income recipients fairly.

Words and concepts are important weapons in the fight against inflation. One of the most important functions of government in the major industrialized nations is to educate the public that the competing demands of groups for increased money incomes is ultimately a fight over the distribution of a nation's total income. In a free market capitalist system, this struggle over the arbitrary and inequitable distribution of income is, in the absence of an incomes policy, likely to be a no-win, actual-lose game for all the nation's citizens, although there may be relative winners for periods of time. It is the responsibility of government to develop a political consensus regarding the desirability of an incomes policy that will distribute the income of a prosperous productive capitalist economy in a civilized manner.

The historical record shows that during the years 1961 to 1968, when the government was able to create a political consensus supporting a policy of directly constraining the money income growth of various groups with some form of a civil incomes policy, the economy approached full-employment prosperity without suffering from inflation.

During these Kennedy-Johnson administration years, prices were held in check by a wage-price "guideline" policy that urged that money-wage rate increases be geared to productivity increases. These guidelines were entirely voluntary. There were no monetary rewards or punishments to force workers and managers to behave. These guidelines, relying solely on the community accepting the responsibility for its money income demands, were enhanced by President Kennedy's stirring inaugural motto: "Ask not what your country can do for you. Ask what you can do for your country." These voluntary guidelines worked for almost eight years; real GDP rose by 34 percent while the Consumer Price Index rose less than 13 percent. With the Vietnam War, however, the civic cohesion generated by Kennedy's charisma was shattered. Compliance with these guidelines disappeared in the last year of the Johnson administration as civic values were degraded and self-interest became a more dominant force.

Thus, there is evidence that a civilized incomes policy can work. In the absence of a sensible civilized policy regarding the distribution of income nationally and internationally, however, the result is not a zero-sum game but a real loss in aggregate income nationally and internationally as governments pursue restrictive monetary and/or fiscal policies and/or permit large businesses to outsource the production of their products.

In today's global economy, where outsourcing has become a significant force in reducing inflationary pressures in industries that can engage in trade as well as a major threat to Western workers' standards of living that contributes to a widening of the inequality of the distribution of income, the call for an incomes policy is rarely heard. If, however, we can resolve the outsourcing problem (as suggested in chapter 7), government will recognize the need for an incomes policy if it accepts the responsibility to encourage and maintain a fully employed, prosperous capitalist economic system.

Chapter 6

AFTER RECOVERY COMES REFORM

In his 1933 open letter to President Roosevelt that was published in the *New York Times*, Keynes recommended that the president develop a strong recovery program as the first priority. After recovery is well under way, the president should work to pass legislation for "business and social reforms which are long overdue." Previous chapters have explained why and what type of recovery program is required for the Keynes Solution to our economic crisis. This chapter and succeeding ones will lay out the kind of business and social reforms that are long overdue and that, I hope, will prevent us from repeating the errors that have led us into the great economic crisis that began in 2007. These needed reforms will make it easier to create a prosperous economic system in the future.

Chapter 1 noted that the origins of the current economic crisis can be traced to the removal of government rules and regulations on the financial system that were installed during the Roosevelt administration. Chapter 2 explained the events leading up to the passage, in 1933, of the Glass-Steagall Act, which separated banking institutions from brokerage firms and investment banks, and how, starting in the 1970s, deregulation of the banking system began. This deregulation culminated with the 1999 repeal of the Glass-Steagall Act, which opened the floodgate for banks and investment bankers to create and organize markets to "securitize" complex mortgage-backed securities such as CDOs (collateralized debt obligations) and SIVs (structured investment vehicles). The investment bankers then told investors that by combining many illiquid mortgages into these mortgage-backed securities, the resulting structured derivative financial instruments were liquid assets that were as good as cash but promised a higher return.

This combining of many illiquid mortgages into exotic financial assets that could then be traded in a market organized by the same investment bankers is called securitization. It was this runaway "securitization" program, propelled by the largest investment banks in America, that led to our current crisis. Alan Greenspan admitted he is at a loss to explain what caused the catastrophic collapse of the organized financial markets where these complex financial assets were traded. Keynes's ideas about the role of money and liquidity in a capitalist system, as discussed in chapter 4, however, provide us with the basis for understanding why this securitization caused the current economic turmoil.

Securitization, Liquidity, and Financial Market Failure[1]

After the repeal of Glass-Steagall, the incentives to originate and quickly sell mortgages, even if borrowers would not normally qualify for the loans, led to the subprime mortgage crisis. By the middle of 2008, governments began to recognize that this crisis threatened the vitality of the private banking system in the United States, the United Kingdom, and many other nations.

Initially known as the U.S. subprime mortgage problem, the difficulties arose as some major investment bankers combined many mortgages, then "sliced and diced" these mortgages, and then blended the pieces into financial derivatives. The rating agencies endorsed underwriters' claims that these were extremely safe, liquid assets. The buyers of these financial derivative assets were people and institutions looking for liquid time machines to move their current purchasing power plus a good return to the indefinite future.

The investment bankers who originated these financial assets also organized the markets in which these securities could be traded. Suddenly in 2007 and 2008, many of these financial assets lost their liquidity, and market values plunged to what has often been called "fire sale prices," if the assets could be sold at all.

This failure of the market to provide holders with an orderly movement in market prices where they could sell their holdings proved contagious. Disorderliness spilled over to other markets, such as the auction-rate securities markets. These auction-rate markets, which had seen few failures before 2008, experienced over a thousand failures in January and February 2008. What caused the failure of these securitized assets and this contagion to spill over and result in a tremendous increase in market failures?

The answer is simple: Economists, financial market regulators, and market participants forgot Keynes's liquidity preference theory and instead swallowed hook, line, and sinker the belief that the classical efficient market theory is a useful model for understanding the operation of real-world financial markets. The efficient market theory suggests that if informed buyers and sellers are brought together in an unregulated, free financial market, the market price will always adjust in an orderly manner to the market clearing price. This market clearing price would be based on market "fundamentals" that represent actuarially "known" profitability from the future cash flows that the underlying mortgages backing these derivative securities will generate. Unfortunately, if the future is uncertain and cannot be reliably predicted on the basis of existing data, then there is no reliable actuarial value that can be assigned. Consequently, what will determine the market price of such securities at any point of time?

In the pre-computer age, in order to ensure that enough buyers and sellers would congregate to do business at a single place, financial markets required buyers and sellers to be represented by dealers who would meet in a physical location (e.g., the stock market) to trade. Members of these stock exchanges, however, recognized that at any given moment of the trading day, there may be a problem of getting a sufficient number of buyers and sellers together to maintain a well-organized and orderly market. It was, therefore, necessary to adopt financial market rules that required all market participants to deal only with authorized broker-dealers who were permitted to execute trades in the market. The broker-dealers acted as fiduciary agents to place orders with other members of the stock exchange, called "specialists" on the New York Stock Exchange. Each specialist kept the books on all buy and sell orders for a specific security at any price.

To ensure that the market price of securities changed in an orderly manner, specialists were expected to act as "market makers" to prevent a disorderly change in the transaction price from the previous price. If, for example, the number of sellers heavily outweighed the number of buyers at any time during the trading day, the specialists were required to buy on their own account in order to try to maintain orderliness in any market price changes (and vice versa if buyers heavily exceeded sellers). Orderliness is a necessary condition to convince holders of the traded asset that they can readily liquidate their position at a market price close to the last publicly announced price. In other words, *orderliness is necessary to maintain liquidity* in these markets.

Modern financial efficient market theory suggests that these quaint institutional arrangements for market maker specialists are antiquated in the computer age. Classical efficient market theory implies that, by using the computer and the Internet, huge numbers of buyers and sellers can meet rapidly and efficiently in virtual space. Consequently, advocates of this theory suggest that there is no need for humans to act as specialists who make the market. Computers can keep the book on buy and sell orders, matching them in an orderly manner, more rapidly and more cheaply than the humans who had done these things in the past.

Underlying this classical efficient market theory is the presumption that the value of traded financial assets is already predetermined by today's market "fundamentals" (at least in the long run[2]), as the earlier quotes from Alan Greenspan and Lawrence Summers suggested.

In many financial markets that have failed, the underlying financial instruments that were to provide the future cash flow for investors typically were long-term debt instruments, such as mortgages or even long-term corporate or municipal bonds. A necessary condition for these markets to be efficient is that the probabilistic risk of the debtors to fail to meet all *future* cash flow contractual debt obligations can be known with actuarial certainty. With this knowledge of the future, one can choose the profit opportunities that best suit one's self-interest.

Classical theorists assume that any observed market price variations around the hypothetical actuarial value (i.e., the price based on market fundamentals) of the traded assets representing these debt instruments is statistical white noise. Any statistician will tell you, if the size of the sample increases, then the variance (i.e., the quantitative measure of the white noise) decreases. In other words, the larger the sample, the closer will be the cluster of actual market prices to the fundamentals-determined market price.

Since computers can bring together many more buyers and sellers globally than the antiquated pre-computer market arrangements, the size of the sample of trading participants in the computer age will rise dramatically. If, therefore, you believe in the classical efficient market theory, then permitting computers to help organize the market will decrease significantly the variance and therefore increase the probability of a more well-organized and orderly market than existed in the pre-computer era.

Consequently, classical efficient market theory advocates such as Alan Greenspan suggest that the spreading of probabilistic risks for holders of these assets is much more efficient and the cost of each transaction is diminished significantly. As I have already noted, underlying this classical efficient market theory is the fundamental belief that the future is known (the ergodic axiom).

For believers in classical efficient market theory, the presumption that there is a plethora of buyers and sellers that can be collected by a computer ensures that the assets being traded are very liquid. In a world of efficient financial markets, therefore, holders of market-traded assets can readily liquidate their position at a price close to the previously announced market price whenever they wish to do so. If this theory is applicable to our world, then how can we explain so many securitized financial markets failing in the sense that investors are finding themselves locked into investments they cannot cash out of?

Why Securitized Markets Failed

Keynes's liquidity theory, as developed in chapter 4, provides the basis for an explanation of why the markets for securitized assets failed and the assets suddenly became illiquid. Keynes argued that the economic future is uncertain and that, therefore, the classical ergodic axiom that is fundamental to any efficient market theory is not applicable to real-world financial markets.

In our world of uncertainty, the primary function of financial markets that trade in resalable assets is to provide liquidity. As chapter 4 noted, the degree of liquidity of the assets traded in any organized market will be enhanced by the existence of credible market makers who attempt to create public confidence in the belief that there will always be an orderly resale market. The existence of market makers suggests to holders that if buyers do not appear to purchase offered securities at an orderly decline in price, the market makers will make their best efforts to maintain orderliness, even if doing so requires them to buy for their own account. In other words, in a market where market makers exist, holders of the asset can be reasonably confident that they can always execute a fast exit strategy and liquidate their position easily.

If market makers cannot support the market with sufficient cash when a cascade of sell orders occurs, the market will fail, and the asset will become virtually illiquid. Trading will be suspended until market makers can rally enough additional support for the buyers' side of the market to reinstate orderliness.

In other words, in a world where the future is uncertain and not just probabilistically risky, for an orderly liquid resale market to exist, *there must be market makers* who assure the public that they will swim against any riptide of sell orders. Thus, market makers must be very wealthy, or at least have access to significant quantities of cash if needed. Nevertheless, any private market maker could exhaust his or her cash reserve in fighting against a cascade of sell orders. Liquidity can be guaranteed under the harshest of market conditions *only* if market makers have easy direct or indirect access to the nation's central bank to obtain the funds necessary to maintain financial market orderliness. Only market makers having such preferred access to the central bank can be reasonably certain that they can *always* obtain enough cash to stem any potential disastrous financial market collapse.

An interesting illustration of this occurred in the days following the terrorist attacks on the World Trade Center and the Pentagon on September 11, 2001. As the World Trade Center buildings collapsed, there was a great fear that the public's confidence in New York financial markets and the U.S. government would also collapse. To maintain confidence in the government bond market in the two days following the attack, the Federal Reserve pumped $45 billion into the banking system. Simultaneously, since the primary bond dealers in New York tend to "make" the government bond market, the *Wall Street Journal* reported shortly after September 11 that "to ease cash concerns among primary dealers in bonds—which include investment banks that are not able to borrow money directly from the Fed—the Fed on Thursday [September 13, 2001] snapped up all the government securities offered by dealers, $70.2 billion worth. On Friday it poured even more into the system, buying a record $81.25 billion of government securities."[3]

In effect, the Fed's buying Treasury debt in exchange for money removed liquid government bonds from many members of the public who, worried about the future after the terrorist attacks, wanted to rid their portfolio of government bonds, while very few members of the public rushed in to buy government bonds. In the days after September 11, the Fed made liquidity available to financial intermediaries that make the government bond market. Any member of the general public who wanted to do so could make a fast exit in an orderly government bond market.

The *Journal* also reported that just before the New York Stock Exchange reopened on September 17 for the first time since the terrorist attack, investment banker Goldman Sachs, loaded with liquidity due to Fed activities, phoned the chief investment officer of a large mutual fund group to say that Goldman was willing to buy any stocks the fund managers wanted to sell. The *Journal* notes that, at the same time, corporations "also jumped in, taking advantage of regulators' newly relaxed stock buyback rules." These corporations bought back securities that the general public held, thereby helping to make the market by propping up the price of their securities.

In a more recent case, on March 13, 2008, the Fed worked out a deal via J.P. Morgan Chase to provide Bear Stearns with a loan against which Bear Stearns pledged as collateral its basically illiquid mortgage-backed securities. This permitted Bear Stearns from having to dump securities on already failing markets in an attempt to obtain enough liquidity to meet its "repo"[4] loan obligations due on March 14. Accordingly, Bear Stearns gained some breathing room, and the selling pressure on financial markets was relieved, at least temporarily. J.P. Morgan was the conduit for the loans to Bear Stearns because Morgan has access to the Fed's discount window and it is supervised by the Fed. Nevertheless, it was obvious on March 13 that if Bear Stearns failed and the collateral was insufficient to cover the loan, it would be the Fed, not J.P. Morgan, that would take the loss.

On the (Sunday) evening of March 16, the Fed and Morgan announced that Morgan would buy Bear Stearns for the fire sale price of $2 per share. (Bear Stearns shares had closed at $30 per share on Friday, March 14.) The Fed also agreed to lend up to $30 billion to Morgan to finance the illiquid assets it inherited from the purchase of Bear Stearns. In essence, the Fed was acting almost like the Resolution Trust Corporation that dealt with the illiquid assets of insolvent savings and loan banks during the 1989 savings and loan insolvency crisis.[5] The Fed's actions prevented J.P. Morgan from having to dump Bear Stearns's assets on the market to meet its inherited obligations.

The post–September 11, 2001, activities of the Federal Reserve vividly demonstrate that the central bank can either directly or indirectly make the market for securities by reducing the outstanding supply of securities available for sale to the general public. The public can then satisfy its increased bearish tendencies by increasing its money holdings without depressing the market price for financial assets in a disorderly manner. Until, and unless, the public's increase in bearishness recedes, the central bank and the market makers can hold that portion of the outstanding liquid assets that the public does not want to own.

In sum, although the existence of a market maker provides, all other things being equal, a higher degree of liquidity for the traded assets, this assurance could dry up in severe sell conditions unless the central bank is willing to take direct action to provide resources to the market maker or, even indirectly, to the market. If the market maker runs down its own resources and is not backed by the central bank indirectly, the asset becomes temporarily illiquid. Nevertheless, the asset holder "knows" that the market maker is providing its best efforts to search to bolster the buyers' side and thereby restore liquidity to the market.

In markets without a market maker, there can be no assurance that the apparent liquidity of an asset cannot disappear almost instantaneously. Moreover, there is nothing to inspire confidence that someone is working to try to restore liquidity to the market.

Those efficient market advocates who suggest that all that is needed is a computer-based organization of a market are assuming that the computer will always search and find enough participants to buy the security whenever a large number of holders want to sell. After all, the white noise of buyers and sellers at prices other than the equilibrium price in efficient markets is assumed to be normally distributed around the fundamentals price. Hence, by assumption, there can never be a shortage of participants on one side or the other of financial markets.

With the failure of thousands of mortgage-backed security markets and auction-rate security markets in the first weeks of February 2008, it is clear that the computers failed to find sufficient buyers to maintain orderliness in these markets. Moreover, computers are not programmed to automatically enter into failing markets and begin purchasing when almost everyone wants to sell at, or near, the last market price. The investment bankers who organize and sponsor the auction-rate securities markets (and the many other securitized markets) will not act as market makers. They may engage in "price talk" before the market opens[6] to suggest to their clients the probable range of the day's market clearing price. These price-talk financial institutions, however, do not put their money where their mouths are. They are not required to try to make the market if the market clearing price is significantly below their price-talk estimate.

Nevertheless, there are many reports that representatives of these investment bankers have told clients that these securitized financial assets "were 'cash equivalents.'" Many holders believed their holdings were very liquid; after all, big financial institutions, such as Goldman Sachs, Lehman Brothers, and Merrill Lynch, were the dealers that organized the markets and normally provided price talk. An article in the February 15, 2008, issue of the *New York Times* reported: "Some well-heeled investors got a big jolt from Goldman Sachs this week; Goldman, the most celebrated bank on Wall Street, refused to let them withdraw money from investments that they considered as safe as cash.... Goldman, Lehman Brothers, Merrill Lynch, etc. have been telling investors the market for these securities is frozen—and so is their cash."[7]

The absence of a credible market maker has shown these assets can easily become illiquid. Had these investors learned the harsh realities of Keynes's liquidity analysis, instead of being seduced by the classical efficient market theory Sirens, they might never have participated in these markets. Should not U.S. security laws and regulations provide sufficient information, so investors could have made an informed decision?

Finally, I should take note of another wrinkle that created additional credit crisis havoc. This involved an innovative financial instrument known as the credit default swap, an instrument that was supposed to provide an insurance policy against default. This instrument was developed by American financial services firms operating under the efficient market belief that the future was statistically predictable, and therefore just as insurable as life insurance and fire insurance were predictable. Accordingly, defaults could be predicted on the basis of past data.

If future outcomes cannot be reliably predicted on the basis of past and present data, however, there is no actuarial basis for the market to provide holders of financial debt assets insurance protection against possible borrower default.

Yet, in recent years, selling these credit default swaps as insurance vehicles has become a huge business. The Commodity Trading Modernization Act of 2000 encouraged development of this financial instrument. The act was rushed through Congress just before Christmas 1999 and signed by President Clinton in January 2000. The act's sponsor, Senator Phil Gramm of Texas, is said to have declared that it would ensure that neither of the two governmental regulatory agencies, the Securities and Exchange Commission and the Commodity Futures Trading Commission, would be able to regulate newly developing exotic financial instruments, especially these credit default swaps. Passage of the act would protect financial institutions from overregulation, Gramm claimed, and the act would position America's financial service institutions to be the world leaders in fostering innovative financial market products.

A credit default swap was sold as if it were an insurance policy. Thus, buyers paid an annual premium equal to a percentage of the outstanding value of the debt-based asset in return for insurance that they would receive payment of the entire value of the amount insured if a default occurred. Since these credit default swaps are unregulated, no agency certifies that the seller of this insurance has enough in reserve to pay off in case of default.

Moreover, because of the lack of regulation, there is no requirement that buyers of this insurance have an "insurable interest"—a position in the particular debt that is being insured against default. Anyone who wants to bet that there is going to be a default apparently can buy a credit default swap—even those with no holdings of the debt instrument being insured. In other words, buyers could place a bet equal to the annual premium of x percent of the value of insurance; if default occurred within the insurance period, the bettors would collect several times the amount of their annual premium bet. Many people took advantage of this loophole, placing bets regarding possible defaults. By 2007, the market for these credit swap derivative assets exceeded $45 trillion—almost four times the size of the entire U.S. stock markets. Obviously, no group of insurance companies could have sufficient reserves to insure such a huge market. But even more important, how would anyone evaluate the reserves necessary for insurance of this $45 trillion market, when these financial markets are governed by nonergodic processes and therefore the incidence of defaults is uncertain and no one can estimate the probabilistic risk of default?

American International Group (AIG), the sixteenth-largest public company in the world and the world's largest insurance company, made a huge business in selling credit default swaps insurance to protect against possible defaults. When defaults occurred, especially in many securitized markets, AIG suffered a liquidity crisis. In September 2008, it was reported that AIG had experienced billions of dollars more in losses than the company had estimated that its losses could total. AIG would not have been able to meet its contractual obligations to credit default holders without the Federal Reserve and the Treasury providing billions of dollars to bail out the company. By February 2009, the government had provided $150 billion to bail out AIG.

If the future cannot be reliably predicted by past market data, as Keynes claimed, then it is impossible to actuarially estimate insurance payouts on credit default swaps. Had the Commodity Modernization Trading Act not deregulated the credit default swap market, state insurance regulators might have been able to stop the sale of these credit default swaps as insurance products for a default event when it is impossible to obtain reliable actuarial estimates of possible losses.

Policy

The government policy response to the failing securitized financial market can be broken into two parts: prevent future recurrences of this widespread failure of public financial markets, and limit the depressing effects of the current credit crunch in these securitized financial markets.

Prevention is the easier of the two responses to discuss.

Prevention of Future Problems

According to the Web page of the Securities and Exchange Commission (SEC): "The mission of the U.S. Securities and

Exchange Commission is to protect investors, maintain fair, orderly, and efficient markets, and facilitate capital formation." The Web page then goes on to note that the Securities Act of 1933 had two basic objectives: "require that investors receive financial and other significant information concerning securities being offered for public sales, and prohibit deceit, misrepresentations, and other frauds in the sale of securities."

The SEC regulations typically apply to public financial markets where the buyer and the seller of an asset do not ordinarily identify themselves to each other. In a public financial market, each buyer purchases from the impersonal market, and each seller sells to the impersonal market. It is the responsibility of the SEC to ensure investors that these public markets are orderly.

In contrast, in a private financial market, both the buyer and the seller of a financial asset are identified to each other. For example, bank loans are typically private market transactions where the bank manager knows the borrower. These bank loans would not come under the purview of the SEC. Under the Glass-Steagall Act, there was no public resale market for securities for these private market bank loans. The issued asset from a transaction in a private market traditionally has been illiquid.

The SEC also declares on its Web page: "As more and more first-time investors turn to the markets to help secure their futures, pay for homes, and send children to college, our investor protection mission is more compelling than ever." Given today's failed and failing public securitized financial markets, it would appear that the SEC has been lax in pursuing its stated mission of investor protection. Accordingly, Congress should require the SEC to enforce diligently two rules:

1. The SEC should require public notice of potential illiquidity for public markets that do not have a credible market maker.
2. The SEC should prohibit any securitization that attempts to create a public market for assets that originated in private markets.

Furthermore, Congress should legislate a twenty-first-century version of the Glass-Steagall Act.

I will discuss these three items in turn. In the last quarter of a century, large financial underwriters have created public markets, which, via securitization, appeared to convert long-term debt instruments (some of them very illiquid, e.g., mortgages) into the virtual equivalent of high-yield, very liquid money market funds and other short-term deposit accounts. As the newspaper reports cited indicate, given the celebrated status of the investment bank underwriters and the statements of their representatives to clients, individual investors were led to believe that they could liquidate their position at an orderly change in price from the publicly announced last transaction price.

This perceived high degree of liquidity for these securitized assets has proven to be illusory. Purchasers might have recognized the potential low degree of liquidity associated with these assets if they had been informed of all the small print regarding market organization. In auction-rate security markets, for example, although organizer-underwriters can buy for their own accounts, they are not obligated to maintain an orderly market. Since the mandate of the SEC is to assure orderly public financial markets and "require that investors receive financial and other significant information concerning securities being offered for public sales, and prohibit deceit [and] misrepresentations…in the sale of securities," it would seem obvious either (1) that all public financial markets organized without the existence of a credible market maker should be shut down because of the potential for disorderliness, or, (2) at a minimum, that information regarding the potential illiquidity of such assets should be widely advertised and made part of essential information that must be given to each purchaser of assets being traded in the securitized market.

Shutting down financial markets that do not have a market maker institution would meet with severe political resistance. The financial community will argue that in a global economy with easy electronic transfers of funds, such a prohibition would merely encourage investors to deal with foreign financial markets and underwriters to the detriment of domestic financial institutions and domestic industries trying to obtain capital funding.

In chapter 8, when discussing needed reforms involving international trade and payment relationships, I develop Keynes's idea on providing an innovative international payments system. The proposed system is a variant of the plan Keynes presented at the Bretton Woods conference in 1944, which was rejected by the United States. If a modern-day version of the Keynes Plan was in operation, it could prevent U.S. residents from trading in foreign financial markets that the United States deemed detrimental to American firms that observed SEC rules while foreign firms did not. If, however, we assume that there is no political will to reform the international payments system and therefore the current system remains in effect, there may still exist a fear in the financial community of loss of jobs and profits for American firms to foreign firms in the financial service industry. In that case, the SEC could permit the existence of public financial markets without credible market makers as long as it required the organizers to clearly advertise the possible loss of liquidity that can occur to holders of assets traded in these markets.

A civilized society does not believe in *caveat emptor* for markets where products are sold that can have adverse health effects. Despite the widespread public information that smoking is a tremendous health hazard, government regulations still require cigarette companies to print in bold letters on each package of cigarettes the warning: "Smoking can be injurious to your health." In a similar manner, any purchases on an organized public financial market that does not have a credible market maker can have serious effects on the financial health of purchasers. Accordingly, the SEC should require this warning to potential purchasers of assets traded in a market without a credible market maker:

This market is not organized by a Securities and Exchange Commission–certified credible market maker. Consequently it may not be possible to sustain the liquidity of the assets being traded. Holders must recognize that they may find that their position in these markets can be frozen and they may be unable to liquidate their holdings for cash.

Furthermore, the SEC should set up strictly enforced rules regarding the minimum amount of financial resources that an entity must possess in order to be certified as a credible market maker for any financial market. The SEC would be required to recertify all market makers periodically, but at least once a year.

To the extent that mutual fund managers who deal with the public wish to participate in financial markets that operate without an SEC-certified credible market maker, the managers must set up a separate mutual fund that deals only in such securities. These specific mutual funds must advertise in bold letters the aforementioned warning—and this warning must be repeated to all investors anytime they make an investment in these funds as well as every time they receive a statement either electronically or by regular mail of their position in the specific mutual fund.

The second rule the SEC should enforce is the prohibition against securitization that attempts to create a public market for assets that originated in private markets (e.g., mortgages, commercial bank loans, etc.). Since the condition and location of the collateral, the creditworthiness of the borrower, and other factors of every home mortgage are so individualized, there is no possible way that investors or rating agencies can evaluate the worth of financial assets that combine many mortgages into one investment vehicle. Accordingly, the prohibition of securitization for such assets is a necessary protection for all investors, just as the Pure Food and Drug Act protects consumers from buying toxic goods that they are incapable of testing on their own.

The third item is that Congress should legislate a twenty-first-century version of the Glass-Steagall Act. The purpose of such an act is to force financial institutions to be either ordinary bank lenders creating loans for individual customers in a private financial market or underwriter brokers who can deal only with instruments created and resold in a public financial market.

I have already noted how the repeal of the Glass-Steagall Act opened the floodgates to securitization and the creation of what some have called a supermarket banking model, where a single financial institution provided a huge range of services: individual banking accounts and loans and investment banking activities, including creating and selling very complex financial market instruments. This supermarket model created the current economic crisis. It also has prevented government efforts from unblocking normal loan channels to permit credit to flow to borrowers who will produce output and create jobs.

The history of the Great Depression shows the need for a new version of Glass-Steagall. Legislation is required to separate and keep independent a strong commercial banking system whose primary function is to provide households with insured bank deposit accounts and loans to qualified borrowers using some measure of qualification based on the old three Cs of banking: collateral, credit history, and character. Bank lenders would have to investigate and know the characters of borrowers and the purpose for which borrowers are requesting the loan. Since deposits at these banks would be insured by a government agency, they would be subject to government regulation, oversight, and strict auditing procedures. Any financial institution that did not meet government rules and regulations under this new legislation would not be permitted to provide bank deposit accounts to the public.

The part of the financial industry required to be legally separated from this commercial banking sector would consist of participants in the public financial markets and would include any institution that took on investment banking functions as well as brokerage firms, hedge funds, and private equity funds. If my previous policy recommendations are adopted, well-organized and orderly financial markets would be separated from those in which there are no market makers; thus, it would be necessary to regulate these noncommercial banking institutions only to the extent that their operations might threaten the orderliness of the financial markets in which they engage. It might be necessary to impose regulations equivalent to margin requirements on these institutions to constrain the amount of leverage they can use to operate in such markets.

Mitigating the Impact of the Current Financial Institution Insolvency Problem

What can be done to mitigate the depressing consequences of the current financial mess?

As early as January 2008, I proposed:

1. the creation of twenty-first-century equivalents of the Roosevelt era Home Owners' Loan Association (HOLC) and the Bush I administration's Resolution Trust Corporation (RTC) to alleviate the U.S. housing bubble crisis and to prevent potential massive insolvency problems; and
2. the need for massive infusions of cash for financial institutions that are too big to fail.

In chapter 2 I briefly discussed how the HOLC operated in the Roosevelt years and how it might operate if revived today.

The RTC was created to resolve the savings and loan (S&L) crisis of 1989—a crisis that, although much smaller in magnitude, has some characteristics similar to today's banking problems. At that time, many S&Ls in search of higher returns made mortgage loans to very questionable borrowers. The result was a sudden increase in default rates that caused a real estate crash. The RTC, created by Congress in 1989 to respond to the insolvency of hundreds of S&Ls in the United States, took over the failing S&Ls, sold off the remaining good assets to other "good," solvent banks, and took onto its own balance sheet the toxic mortgage loan assets of the insolvent ones. The RTC would hold these assets and sell them only when there was a reasonable market price for them. The result was to rebuild the idea that the remaining S&Ls were good banks.

The RTC was created during a Republican administration that had pledged "no new taxes." Nevertheless, recognizing the severity of the problem and the large number of S&L insolvencies, President George H. W. Bush supported the formation of the RTC. Apparently this administration recognized that the RTC would not require new taxes to burden the U.S. taxpayer. The alternative, doing nothing, could result in an economic disaster. In 1995, the RTC was folded into a larger government agency, the Savings Association Insurance Fund of the Federal Deposit Insurance Corporation. No public accounting records have been provided to show whether the RTC operations ultimately made a profit or a loss.

In sum, setting up an institution such as the RTC involves some accounting costs, but these bookkeeping entries are unlikely to hurt taxpayers significantly. The benefits of such an institution to alleviate economic distress far outweigh the cost of allowing deflationary market forces to solve the problem of our burst housing and financial bubble.

Although the problem of insolvent financial institutions is much greater than it was during the S&L crisis, there is still a need for the establishment of a government institution to remove the toxic assets from the marketplace by taking them off the balance sheets of the many large banking institutions that face insolvency. By buying the troubled assets, this government agency would be operating in a role similar to the central bank, which acts as the market maker of last resort.

Of course, the problem of evaluating these toxic assets and determining what price to pay for absorbing them remains. The original plan that Secretary of the Treasury Henry Paulson sent to Congress in September 2008 was only three pages long. It would have given the Treasury secretary the right to buy these toxic illiquid assets at any price he decided was correct, provided the price did not to exceed that which the holder originally paid. This action would improve the balance sheets of any financial institutions holding toxic assets and remove any fear of insolvency. But it also was politically impractical, for it meant that neither management nor stockholders would bear any loss due to their errors in creating and/or purchasing these exotic financial assets in the first place.

The question, which cannot be easily answered, remains: What price should a resurrected Resolution Trust Corporation–type government agency pay for these toxic assets? To what extent should current stockholders of financial institutions facing insolvency because of toxic asset holdings be required to take what Wall Street calls a "haircut"? In other words, how much of a loss should these stockholders take when the institutions sell these assets to the government agency? What price between a fire sale price and the price the corporation initially paid to purchase the toxic assets should the government agency pay?

The determination of such a price is beyond the scope of this book, just as a Keynes Solution would not try to evaluate the penalty for a driver exceeding the speed limit. Clearly the price should not be so low as to cause a collapse of the entire banking system, nor should it be so high as to reward management and stockholders despite their errors.

Some have recommended that the government should follow Sweden's lead during its banking crisis of the 1990s. In the Swedish case, government placed faltering banks into what was called a "bad bank," where the troubled assets were to be held until some future time when the economy and markets improved and the public was willing to buy the assets back.

The government "paid" for these bad assets by injecting sufficient funds into the bank to recapitalize it. The existing stockholders were basically wiped out. The result was a temporary "nationalization" of banks. But the restored banks could resume making loans. The government held and managed these bad assets, hoping to get as reasonable a price as possible in the future. When the market and the economy improved, the market for these bad assets also improved.

Whether the government agency takes a major stake in banks or not, the revived RTC, by warehousing bad assets, would maintain liquidity in the financial system despite the public's increase in bearishness. In other words, this government agency would hold that portion of the outstanding financial assets that the public does not want to own.

Whether the United States actually needs to nationalize its bad banks or whether it can merely take a sufficient equity position to make sure banks receiving government funds resume making loans is more of a political question than an economic one. The important thing is to recognize that by buying up these troubled assets that are no longer liquid, the government is restoring a modicum of liquidity to the economic system. And as Keynes insisted, a capitalist system needs liquidity to function.

If the government agency holds these troubled assets as long as necessary and until the public is willing to invest in them, then these assets cannot be an undue burden to the financial system. Thus, a revived version of an RTC-type government-sponsored institution in tandem with a revived version of the HOLC will rectify the problems haunting the U.S. housing market. Although in January 2008, I had hoped that quick policy action could solve the housing problem and avoid a recession, by 2009, it is obvious that any move in this direction is too late to avoid recession. Moreover, the size of the rescue package needed to solve the housing problem and remove a sufficient number of toxic assets to restore confidence in the banking system has risen and will continue to rise every day that some positive action is not taken.

Nevertheless, Keynes's ideas about the operation of a capitalist economy still suggest that reviving a twenty-first-century version of HOLC and RTC can mitigate the problems in which we are enmeshed. The longer the administration delays, however, the deeper the hole that we must extract ourselves from.

Chapter 7

REFORMING INTERNATIONAL TRADE

Mainstream classical theorists aver that a policy of free trade and freely flexible exchange rates will provide an era of abundance for all the citizens of the nation. In this context, "free trade" means that governments do not interfere in the importation of goods and services either by placing tariffs (taxes) on imports or by limiting the amount of a product that can be imported into the country (i.e., by imposing import quotas). Freely flexible exchange rates require a free market unfettered by any government intervention to determine the purchase price of a foreign currency in terms of the domestic money. Moreover, the government cannot impose any restrictions or limitations on the amount of foreign currency a resident can purchase or limit the amount of domestic currency that a foreigner buys.

Since the 1970s, whether the Democrats or the Republicans were in control of Congress and/or the White House, the U.S. government has advocated—or at least paid lip service to—the desirability of the government entering into free trade agreements (e.g., the North American Free Trade Agreement) with other nations. Furthermore, the U.S. government has not directly intervened in the foreign exchange markets.

If you believe this classical efficient market theory argument regarding international trade and payments, then you would think that after more than three decades of the government pursuing these classical theory objectives, the U.S. trade and payments relationships with the rest of the world would be free of any problems.

Unfortunately, several unpleasant economic things have happened to the United States on the international economics front during this period. First, the United States, despite being the biggest economy in the world, has become the world's largest debtor. Second, many U.S. residents have seen their high-wage jobs outsourced to low-wage nations. As Louis Uchitelle, the *New York Times* Financial Page reporter, documents in his 2006 book *The Disposable American: Layoffs and Their Consequences*, these workers whose jobs are outsourced experienced severe damage to their self-esteem and therefore to their mental health. In some cases, this led to marital breakups and other serious personal consequences.

The Bureau of Labor Statistics data Uchitelle used indicated that, two years later, only one of every three laid-off workers ended up earning in a new job as much or more than they did in the lost job. The other two-thirds of the displaced workers earned significantly less or were still not employed; some even had stopped looking for a job. Moreover, in general, the impact of outsourcing was to put downward pressure on those who remained employed in jobs similar to the ones that had been outsourced.

The existence of a large number of outsourced workers looking for jobs tends to depress the wages of all other workers in an area, even if those still employed are in industries where outsourcing is less likely to occur. Consequently, it is not surprising that money wages in the United States have stagnated over the last few decades, and the inequality of the income distribution has become greater as more and more blue-collar jobs have been outsourced in the name of free trade.

Nevertheless, mainstream economists still claim that free trade and freely flexible exchange rates promote maximum efficiency and prosperity globally. For example, in the spring of 2005, the then chairman of President Bush's Council of Economic Advisors, Harvard professor N. Greg Mankiw, defended the practice of "outsourcing" production where American firms, instead of hiring residents to work in factories located in the United States, shift production to factories overseas where lower-wage workers are readily available. Mankiw claimed that, despite the obvious loss of high-wage jobs by American workers to lower-wage foreign workers, outsourcing is beneficial to both the U.S. economy and the rest of the world. Mankiw argues that, *in the long run*, free trade will result in more income and wealth for all nations by creating new higher-value jobs for workers in the United States as well as the jobs in the nations to which production has been outsourced.

Of course, one response to the Mankiw proclamation is Keynes's old phrase: "In the long run we will all be dead." And the outsourced disposable workers are likely to die even earlier. Keynes's analysis of the operation of a monetary economy suggests why the argument propagated by mainstream classical economists regarding desirability of outsourcing is wrong. According to Keynes, the claim that prosperity is inevitable if only we permit free trade can be "misleading and dangerous." Clearly the evidence supports Keynes's view and not Mankiw's mainstream classical economic theory proclamation.

Why is there such an obvious disparity between what classical theory claims are the universal benefits of trade and the observed hardships to American workers due to trade based on outsourcing of jobs?

In this chapter I discuss why the classical free trade argument is not applicable to the world that we inhabit. I also explain what reforms should be put in place to ensure that trade benefits all workers in a civilized capitalist system. In chapter 8 I discuss the Keynes alternative to a freely flexible exchange rates system and explain why reforming the current international payments system toward the Keynes Solution alternative will be beneficial.

Comparative Advantage as the Basis for the Free Trade Argument

One universal economic "truth" that *all* mainstream economists agree on is something that economists call the "law of comparative advantage." If all nations permit free trade, it is claimed that the law of comparative advantage assures that more goods and services will be produced globally as resources in every nation are fully employed. The resulting hypothesized cornucopia of goods and services is obtained by each nation specializing in production in industries in which it has a "comparative advantage" and exporting some of the products of those industries in exchange for imports from the comparative-advantage industries of other nations. As a result, classical theory asserts, all nations should gain from free trade.

What do economists mean by an industry having a comparative advantage? In 1819, the economist David Ricardo introduced the law of comparative advantage to justify the importance of free trade among nations. In Ricardo's view, each nation should specialize in producing for export products from a domestic industry that has the greatest production cost advantage compared to the production costs of producing the identical product in any other nation. Those nations with no industries that have an absolute production cost advantage vis-à-vis industries in other nations producing the same products, Ricardo argued, would gain a "comparative advantage" by exporting products from their industries that have the smallest cost disadvantage. A trade pattern between exports and imports based on Ricardo's comparative advantage principle, it is argued, would permit the wealth of both trading nations to improve as demand for goods and services increases and global output grows to meet this increased demand.

Let us illustrate this law of comparative advantage with a hypothetical example. Assume there are two economies, the East (cheap-labor countries such as India and China) and the West (high-cost-labor countries such as the United States or Western Europe). For simplicity, before free trade begins, assume each economy produced two tradable products—say bicycles (which uses cheap unskilled labor) and computers (which requires higher-paid skilled labor). Assume there is full employment in both economies. Before trade begins, let us assume there are one million fully employed workers in the East and 100,000 fully employed workers in the West engaged in these two industries and that the global total of these 1.1 million employed workers produces (and presumably their employers profitably sell) a total of 375,000 bicycles and 55,000 computers in the marketplace.

According to classical Ricardian theory, the introduction of free trade between East and West will encourage each economy to specialize in producing the products in which it has a comparative advantage. Suppose, using the same production technology in both countries, the East could produce both bicycles and computers at a lower money cost than the West since even the highly skilled workers necessary to produce computers in the East were willing to work for a significantly lower wage than that of highly paid skilled workers in the West. Suppose, however, that because of the lower wages paid to all workers in the East, the East's low cost of production advantage was greater in the bicycle industry than in the computer industry. Economists would say that although the East had an absolute cost advantage in the production of both bicycles and computers—that is, the East can produce both bicycles and computers at a lower money cost than the West can—the East's comparative advantage is in the production of bicycles and the West's comparative advantage (i.e., lower cost disadvantage) is in the production of computers. Then, according to the law of comparative advantage, the East should specialize by employing all its one million workers and capital in the production of bicycles while the West should employ its 100,000 workers and all its capital in specializing in the production of computers.

Assume that because of this specialization, the globally employed 1.1 million workers would produce more bicycles and more computers, say, 400,000 bicycles and 70,000 computers.

In this hypothetical comparative advantage example, by engaging in free trade, it is assumed that the world gained a total of 25,000 additional bicycles and 15,000 additional computers. Then the East should sell bicycles to the West and in turn buy computers from the West. With the same employed labor force before and after trade, by assumption, more of both goods are produced and available for consumption globally. Consequently, the residents of each nation should gain somewhat from this trade; they will have more bicycles and computers for their use while all the goods were produced with the assumed same amount (real cost) of labor time worked in each nation. Thus, it is claimed that the law of comparative advantage "proves" that the real income of the global economy has increased with free trade as more goods and services are provided to consumers in both the East and the West.

For Ricardo, each nation's comparative advantage typically was associated with its unique supply environment (e.g., availability of mineral deposits, climate differences and their effects on agricultural production, etc.) that resulted in differences in production costs. In contrast, our hypothetical example illustrating the argument for "free" trade is based on the notion that opening the domestic market to a foreign source that has lower costs of production is not due to some real productivity advantage such as the workers in the East producing many more bicycles per hour than workers in the West in the bicycle industry. By assuming that the same technology is used in each nation, we are assuming that workers in, say, the bicycle industry in the

West produce as many bicycles per hour of labor time as workers in the bicycle industry in the East. Accordingly, the East's absolute cost advantage in the production of bicycles and computers is simply due to the fact that lower money wages per hour are paid to the workers in the East.

Divergences in real production costs are obvious in agriculture and mineral exploitation, where climate and the nonrandom deposits of minerals among nations make certain commodities relatively cheaper to produce in one country than another. For example, a barrel of oil is cheaper to produce in the Saudi Arabian desert than in the Death Valley desert of the United States mainly because nature has provided significantly more easily obtainable crude oil underground in Saudi Arabia than in Death Valley.

In mass production industries, however, differences in production costs are less likely to reflect differences due to a nation's climatic or mineral endowment, as the same technology is used in production of any specific product in any nation.

Keynes recognized this possibility when he wrote:

A considerable degree of international specialization is necessary in a rational world in all cases where it is indicated by wide differences in climate [and] natural resources....But over an increasingly wide range of industrial products...I become doubtful whether the economic costs of self-sufficiency are great enough to outweigh the other advantage of gradually bringing the producer and the consumer within the same ambit of the same national economic and financial organisations [to ensure full employment]. Experience accumulates to prove that most modern mass production processes can be performed in most countries and climates with equal efficiency.[1]

In other words, Keynes was arguing—and today's facts tend to demonstrate—that, given the existence of multinational firms and the ease with which they can transfer technology internationally, any differences in relative costs of production in most industries are more likely to reflect national differences in money wages (per same hour of "real" human labor) plus the costs of providing "civilized" working conditions, such as limiting the use of child labor, plus the costs to the enterprise of workers' fringe benefits, such as providing health insurance and pension benefits for employees. In today's free trade system, the global location of industrial export factories is more likely to reflect differences in hourly money wages plus occupational safety and other labor fringe benefit expenses that the nation has decided should be borne by enterprise directly rather than by the nation's tax system or that the nation has decided should not be provided to workers.

In the twenty-first century, low transportation and/or communication costs make it possible to deliver many goods and services cheaply to distant foreign markets. Consequently, mass production industries that use low-skilled, semiskilled, or even highly skilled workers are likely to locate factories in those nations where the economic system values human life the lowest, at least as measured by the wage paid per hour of labor and the work environment provided by entrepreneurs. Most developed nations long ago passed legislation that made "sweatshop" production and the use of child labor illegal. Yet such conditions still exist in the "competitive" export industries of most less developed nations. Consequently, free trade competition usually implies that in developed nations, there will be a loss of jobs to workers in nations that have large populations of cheap available labor, working in sweatshops, with little legislation requiring safe and healthy working conditions. The result of such free trade competitive forces must inevitably lower the standard of living of the workers in the developed nations as their wages are reduced toward the wages paid in low-wage countries. Do we really want to reduce the wages of American workers to less than a dollar per hour and simultaneously permit American children to work in factories, as Chinese children do, so that the family can earn enough to avoid starvation?

If we permitted China to build a factory in California and operate it as the factory would be operated in China with (1) children under 14 years old working in the factory; (2) no occupational safety standards; (3) workers on the job for 55 to 60 or more hours a week, at a money-wage rate significantly less than the government-mandated minimum hourly wage in the United States; and (4) the factory polluting the environment, then the civilized laws of the United States would not permit any U.S. resident to buy any products from this California-based Chinese factory. Nevertheless, under the banner of free trade, we permit Americans to buy products from such uncivilized and unhealthy factory environments just because the factories are located in China.

Why should we abandon our belief in the social desirability of a factory system that treats workers in a humane and civilized manner? If we permitted American entrepreneurs to hire workers under the same conditions that Chinese workers are employed, American factories could undersell the factories located in China if only due to lower transportation costs.

Under current conditions, free trade with low-wage nations is not free competitive trade at all since U.S. law prohibits American entrepreneurs from matching Chinese labor hiring and working conditions.

The Keynes Solution to outsourcing jobs to such unfair competitive foreign factories would be to prohibit imports from any factory that did not, at least, meet all the conditions that our labor laws impose on American enterprises. We should also require that all products produced in a foreign nation can be imported only if the goods produced would pass government inspection under the Pure Food and Drug Act and any other consumer protection laws.

Under the current free trade system, there will be little outsourcing of American jobs in those production processes that provide goods and services for the American market where (1) communication and/or transportation costs from foreign nations are very high (e.g., personal services, such as servants, waiters, barbers, nannies, etc.) and (2) immigration legislation limits the importation of cheap labor. Significant employment opportunities still may exist especially in the personal service industries of developed nations with civilized working condition standards. If, however, we continue to permit, under the banner of free trade, the outsourcing of mass production jobs, there is bound to be a growing number of disposable workers from previously high-paying mass production industries looking for any employment opportunities. Consequently, there will be increased competition among these displaced workers for the existing service jobs in nontradable production industries. The result, as Uchitelle's book suggests, will be to depress wages in these nontradable production activities or at least to prevent the wages of employed workers from rising significantly over time. Given the large volume of outsourcing that has occurred in recent years, it is no wonder that the share of wages in U.S. gross domestic product was, by 2005, at its lowest level in decades.

As we crossed the threshold into the twenty-first century, it is clear that the argument for free international trade as a means of promoting the wealth of all nations and their inhabitants cannot be rationalized on the basis of Ricardo's law of comparative advantage—except perhaps for minerals, agriculture, and other industries where value productivity is related to climatic conditions or mineral availability. Production in these particular industries, however, is often controlled by the market power of cartels and/or government policies of producer nations that are designed to prevent market prices from falling sufficiently to reflect the "real" costs of production. In other words, industries for which the law of comparative advantage still might be applicable often are largely sheltered from international competitive forces by the exercise of cartel power (e.g., the Organization of Petroleum Exporting Countries) or government power to control supplies sold on international markets.

The growth of multinational corporations in mass production industries and the movement toward a more liberalized free trade in the final decades of the twentieth century encouraged American business enterprises to "outsource" production—to search for the lowest-wage foreign workers available in order to reduce production costs. The availability of outsourcing also acted as a countervailing power to high-cost, labor union–organized domestic workers in developed countries. Indeed, in the early years of the twenty-first century, the rapidly developing industrial structure of many nations can be attributed largely to the desire of multinational firms to rid themselves of union problems by utilizing low-wage foreign workers to produce identical goods and services using the same technological production processes.

In the early decades after World War II, when transportation and communication costs between nations were large and there were significant restrictions on trade, high domestic unit labor costs spurred entrepreneurs in mass production industries to find innovative ways to improve domestic productivity and thereby reduce labor costs per unit of output. With the growth of multinationals and the removal of many restrictions on the international trading of mass-produced manufactured goods, high domestic labor costs now encourage outsourcing rather than productivity-enhancing investments to lower unit production costs. Under current conditions, it is cheaper to outsource than to search for technological improvements in production processes to reduce unit production costs domestically. Accordingly, unlike what occurred in the past, when technological innovations by entrepreneurs looking to increase output and profitable sales while lowering the unit labor costs raised living standards of all members of a capitalist economy, the higher profits from outsourcing have not been plowed back into research and technological development of domestic production techniques.

Under the rules of free trade today, managers have less of an incentive to pursue innovations to improve domestic labor productivity in any industrial sectors where inexpensive foreign labor can "do the job" and transportation and/or communication costs are small relative to production costs. The decline in the rate of growth of domestic labor productivity in many developed nations since the 1970s can be related, at least in part, to this phenomenon of using cheap foreign labor rather than improving domestic production processes.

The Keynes Solution to the problem of outsourcing, which merely substitutes low-wage workers employed in sweatshop conditions for highly paid workers in a civilized productive environment, is to level the playing field. For any nation such as the United States, whose laws encourage the civilized treatment of workers in domestic factories, imports that are permitted into the country must meet the same legislative labor, environmental, and consumer safety standards that the United States demands of American business firms.

Accordingly, the use of comparative advantage analysis as a justification for letting free markets determine outsourcing, trade, and international payments flows can be, as Keynes warned, "misleading and dangerous" to the health of civilized nations' economies, especially those that restrict the use of child labor, provide their workers with civilized working conditions, and simultaneously provide a high-wage standard of living.

A Second Problem Regarding Comparative Advantage

Unfortunately, the law of comparative advantage requires at least two basic assumptions that are not applicable to the real world in which we live. First, our hypothetical bicycle-computer example assumed that the additional produced supply of 25,000 bicycles and 15,000 computers automatically would create additional global market demand for these products. In other words, the additional bicycles and computers could be sold readily at profitable prices. Wouldn't the multinational auto companies be glad to know that if they increase global productive capacity by placing plants in countries that have comparative advantages in auto assembly, they will sell (at a profit) all the cars they can produce? There can never be surplus capacity—as there seems to be today, in products not only of the big three American automobile companies, but also of the highly regarded Asian automobile firms.

This classical assumption that there will never be any shortage of demand for additional production occurring due to nations specializing in their comparative advantage is, of course, in violation of the facts. This assumption would have to presume that full employment of labor and capacity would automatically occur in all the nations of the global economy in a world of free trade and free markets domestically and internationally. The history of capitalist economies over the past two and a half centuries has shown that most nations rarely achieve full employment; no nation in the world has achieved full employment perpetually. Consequently, if there is anything that economists should have learned since Keynes, it is that you cannot prove that all trading economies will automatically share gains from free trade unless you can be assured that there is full employment in all nations, both before and after free trade.

That brings us to a second problem. It is assumed that the gains from trade due to the law of comparative advantage occur only if *neither capital nor labor* is mobile across national boundaries. In fact, our simple bicycle-computer example indicated that there was no migration of capital or labor between East and West while the law of comparative advantage determined what the exporting industry was in each nation.

If capital is internationally mobile, however, and if, after trade, there is not global full employment, then the beneficial results stemming from the law of comparative advantage need not occur. With free international capital mobility and free trade, entrepreneurs will invest in plant and equipment to produce goods wherever it is most profitable to do so—in other words, where unit labor costs are lowest.[2] Thus, if multinational firms can shift technology from nation to nation so that it will take the same number of man-hours of input to produce a unit of output in each country—or, as Keynes wrote, if "modern mass production processes can be performed in most countries…with equal efficiency"—then capital will always seek nations where labor costs are lower, as that will enhance profit margins.

In our hypothetical example, the East can have the absolute cost advantage in that its unit money labor costs are lower for the production of both bicycles and computers at all relevant ranges of production that the global market can absorb. The East ultimately will attract enough foreign capital to produce all the bicycles and computers necessary to meet global demand. In other words, as long as after-trade demand is not sufficient to ensure global full employment, international production and trade patterns will be determined by the absolute cost advantage of having a large supply of low-wage workers available, not by economists' law of comparative advantage. Consequently, in the West, production and employment in the tradable goods industries will decline substantially, if not completely. In the extreme, most jobs that will remain in the West will be those that cannot be outsourced because high transportation and communication costs outweigh the cheap costs of foreign workers.

Of course, some proponents of comparative advantage theory, such as Mankiw, have an almost religious faith in the belief that despite the loss of high-wage, semiskilled U.S. manufacturing jobs due to outsourcing, the United States will develop (unspecified) higher-skilled jobs in some advanced technology sector while the labor force in China and India will not have sufficient skills or education to be competitive in this new technology sector. Mankiw's long-run qualification that outsourcing is good for the U.S. economy assumes that unemployment will not be a significant problem; he has faith that the new higher-skilled jobs will appear miraculously in the United States.

Why, then, have two-thirds of Uchitelle's disposable workers not found these new high-value jobs? According to conventional wisdom, it is the displaced workers' own fault for having skills that make them eligible only for lower-paying, less productive jobs. In another blame-the-victims-for-their-problems argument, we are often told that unemployed or displaced workers need only to pursue more education, and they will always get a better job. A call for better-educated workers as the remedy for displacement by outsourcing is a measure of a mind that has not thought through the problems of trade patterns in a freely trading global economy where child labor, unsafe working conditions, environmentally damaging production, and a host of other factors not acceptable in the developed world are permitted. In the long run, given the current international payments system and liberalized trade structure plus the obvious lack of full employment among most of the trading nations of the world, it follows that employment in the advanced economies of the world will be concentrated in jobs where transportation and communication costs make foreign trade prohibitive (nontradables) and niche industries, such as defense, where political or social reasons prevent the outsourcing of production.

Since labor in developed nations is more highly valued than in the less developed nations such as China and India, free trade in the products of mass production industries has the potential to impoverish a significant portion of the developed nations' workers. Unless developed nations' governments take deliberate action to secure and maintain full employment of their workers, free trade may ultimately result either in rising rates of unemployment or in their workers being forced to accept real wages that are competitive with wages being paid to low-wage workers in less developed nations. Surely Western politicians should be made aware of these potential "disastrous" results that can occur from blindly applying the classical efficient market theory to today's problem of job outsourcing with liberalized trade and international financial markets. Unless Western governments take strong, positive, direct actions to ensure continuous full employment of their domestic labor force, free trade and outsourcing will not be the panaceas their advocates claim.

Chapter 8

REFORMING THE WORLD'S MONEY

In chapter 4, I indicated that increases in spending create additional profit opportunities that encourage business firms to expand labor hiring. It was implicitly assumed that the additional spending would come from domestic households, business firms, and/or government and would be used to purchase the output produced by factories located in the domestic economy.

Once we open the analysis to a globalized market system, things change somewhat. For example, spending by U.S. households, business firms, and/or government to purchase products produced in foreign nations (i.e., imports) will create profit opportunities and jobs in the foreign nations, not in the domestic economy. In other words, demand for imported goods and services creates jobs in other nations. Demand by foreigners for the products of our domestically located factories (i.e., exports) creates profits and jobs for workers in the domestic economy.

If, in any year, U.S. exports approximately equal the imports into the United States, then the foreign-job-creating effects of

U.S. imports and domestic job creation in U.S. export industries will approximately offset each other. If, however, the United States imports significantly more than it exports, American spending will support more profit opportunities and jobs in foreign nations while the profits of and jobs in U.S. factories will be less than either if exports equaled imports or if all the excess demand for imports over exports had been diverted to a market demand for these same products produced by American factories.

For example, in 2008, the United States imported $677 billion more from foreign nations than it exported. If Americans had spent that $677 billion on goods and services produced in the United States, it would have provided a big stimulus to the American economy. That $677 billion is approximately 90 percent of the amount of government spending and tax cuts provided for in the stimulus bill that President Obama signed in February 2009—a spending bill that is supposed to preserve several million U.S. jobs.

Since 1982, the United States has consistently imported more than it has exported, thereby creating more profit opportunities and jobs in foreign nations than foreigners have been creating in the U.S. export industries. As a result, the United States has acted as the engine for economic growth for the rest of the world for the last quarter of a century. The impressive growth rates displayed by Japan in the 1980s and China and India in the early years of the twenty-first century are based on U.S. increases in spending on exports from these nations.

A simple example will illustrate. Let us assume that in any one year, the United States spends $10 billion more on Chinese imports (say, toys) and therefore $10 billion less on domestically produced toys. Assume that China does not increase spending on U.S. exports and therefore the U.S. trade deficit with China increases by $10 billion. The effect is that this $10 billion spent on imports has created profits and jobs in the Chinese toy industry while U.S. residents who have diverted their spending on domestically produced toys to foreign-produced toys have, in essence, destroyed profits and jobs in the U.S. toy industry.

In this hypothetical example, China has earned $10 billion more on its international trade account. We have assumed that China did not spend this $10 billion buying more American-made products but has "saved" $10 billion out of its international earnings. Since in the Keynes analysis "a penny saved is a penny that cannot be earned," in this example, the $10 billion the Chinese saved is $10 billion that cannot be earned by businesses located in the United States and by American workers.

When imports exceed exports, a deficit in the trade balance exists that economists call an unfavorable balance of trade. This unfavorable trade balance can result in a deficit in the balance of payments between the importing country and the rest of the world as the country pays out more for its imports than it receives in payments for its exports—a $10 billion deficit in our hypothetical toy example. Any nation experiencing a deficit in its international balance of payments must finance this deficit in one of two ways:

1. The deficit nation draws down its previous savings on international earnings (these savings are called the nation's "foreign reserves") to pay for its excess of imports.
2. The deficit nation borrows funds from the rest of the world to pay for the difference between the value of what it imports and the value of what it exports.

Since U.S. imports have exceeded exports every year for the last 25 years, the country has had to borrow from foreigners in order to finance its excess of imports over exports for many years. As a result, the United States has moved from being the world's largest creditor nation to being the largest debtor nation in terms of debt owed to the rest of the world.

To continue with the earlier example, let us consider what the Chinese do with their $10 billion savings on international earnings. Like all savers, the Chinese look for liquid time machines to move their saved (unused) international contractual settlement (purchasing) power to the future. For the most part, the Chinese have used their international savings to purchase U.S. Treasury securities and other debt obligations of U.S. government–sponsored corporations. This fact indicates that the Chinese believe the U.S. dollar is the safest harbor for storing their unused international contractual settlement power. This savings by the Chinese has led many "experts" to say that the Chinese have been financing the American consumer shopping spree and the resulting growing U.S. international debt. If the Chinese stop buying U.S. securities with their international savings, these experts warn, American consumers could no longer afford to buy imports and would have to stop buying so many Chinese-made goods.

If Americans did stop buying so many Chinese imports, it would devastate the profits of Chinese firms and threaten the jobs of Chinese workers. The result could cause political unrest in China. The Chinese Communist Party enjoys popular support as long as it not only protects the nation from foreign enemies, but also continues to take economic actions that result in substantial improvement in living conditions for all its citizens. If Chinese exports decline, then Chinese living standards will drop, which could induce demonstrations and political unrest. In other words, it is unlikely to be in the ruling party's interest to stop financing Americans' huge import bill from China.

Suppose the Chinese spent the $10 billion on the products of American industries, instead of using their international savings to buy Treasury bonds. The result would be that (1) more products from American factories would be available in China to enhance the standard of living of Chinese workers, and (2) American businesses and their workers would earn more income and not have to borrow from the Chinese to finance their excessive import purchases of Chinese goods. The moral of this illustration is that if the Chinese bought goods from the United States instead of buying Treasury bonds, then not only would the Chinese improve the Chinese real living standards even more, but Americans would have enough earnings to afford all the Chinese imports we bought without having to go into debt to the Chinese.

This simple illustration should provide a hint to the Keynes Solution for ending trade imbalances that cause nations with unfavorable balances of trade to incur huge international debts. Later in this chapter I suggest a proposal for instituting such a solution.

In contrast, the classical efficient market theory solution to this trade imbalance problem is to suggest that if the Chinese currency (the yuan) was traded in a free flexible foreign exchange market and the United States ran an unfavorable balance of trade with the Chinese, then the yuan would increase substantially in value relative to the dollar. The cost of Chinese imports in terms of U.S. dollar prices would increase dramatically, until Americans could no longer afford to buy very much from the Chinese; thus, Chinese imports to the United States would decline significantly. With the appreciation of the yuan relative to the dollar, the Chinese would experience a decline in the cost of U.S. imports, and they would buy more imports from the United States.

For technical reasons (known as the Marshall-Lerner conditions) that I need not discuss here, it is possible that even with a decline in the value of the U.S. dollar relative to the Chinese yuan, the value of the trade imbalance between China and the United States would not disappear. In the worst-case scenario, the trade imbalance could actually worsen. I will ignore this possible real-world complication in the discussion that follows. Instead, I will discuss another possible deleterious effect of this classical theory solution to trade imbalances where free markets are always supposed to solve any trade imbalance problem by devaluing the currency of the country experiencing an unfavorable balance of trade.

If, in a free flexible exchange rate market, the value of the U.S. dollar declined relative to the yuan, then the dollar price of Chinese imports at American retail outlets would increase significantly. The immediate result would be that the rate of inflation as measured by the Consumer Price Index would rise because imports are a significant portion of the American consumer budget.

If the Federal Reserve believes that its primary obligation is to fight inflation, then its anti-inflationary policy would require it to increase the domestic interest rate until some low target rate of inflation, say 2 percent, was restored. A rise in interest rates in the United States would destroy some existing profit opportunities for American businesses and increase unemployment in the nation. The goal of the Fed's anti-inflation monetary policy is to reduce the incomes of Americans sufficiently so that American households reduce their purchases of all goods and services, imports from China as well as products from American factories. If its anti-inflation policy is successful, the decline in market demand will act as a brake on rising prices, including imports from China, as Americans buy fewer imports. This reduction in imports would probably slow the appreciation of the yuan relative to the dollar and thereby have some impact on reducing the measured rate of inflation over time.

In this scenario, as Americans buy fewer Chinese imports, profits and jobs in China's export industries would be reduced, creating unemployment and potential political unrest in China. With the loss of jobs in China, the Chinese market demand for U.S. exports should decline, resulting in fewer profit opportunities in American export industries due to the ongoing devaluation of the dollar. Clearly such a scenario is good for neither American nor Chinese workers and business firms.

Classical theory avoids this possible unpleasant scenario by assuming that with free efficient markets, there will *always* be full employment of capital and labor in all trading nations, no matter what changes occur in the exchange rate of currencies between nations. In other words, classical theory merely assumes away this possible unemployment problem. In the long run, classical theory asserts as a matter of faith rather than as empirical evidence, there *must* be full employment in all nations.

By loading the classical model with sufficient but unrealistic axioms, the theory resolves any potential trade deficit problem merely by invoking the magic of free markets for foreign exchange of currencies in a world where the future is known at least in the long run.

Some more pragmatic economists have noted that historically, when exchange rates have been permitted to change freely in the market, the results often have been devastatingly bad for the nation. Consequently, some experts have advocated a foreign exchange market where a market maker actually fixes the exchange rate at some preannounced level. As a result, very often, economic discussions on the requirements for a good international payments system have been limited to this question of the advantages and disadvantages of fixed versus flexible exchange rates.

The facts of experience since the end of World War II, however, and Keynes's revolutionary liquidity analysis indicate that more is required than merely deciding whether exchange rates should be fixed or freely flexible. A mechanism must be designed to adequately resolve persistent trade and international payments imbalances that can occur whether exchange rates are fixed or flexible. The mechanism should be designed not only to resolve these imbalance problems but also simultaneously to promote global full employment. Such a mechanism is embedded in the Keynes Solution for international trade and payment imbalances.

The Bretton Woods Solution

As World War II was winding down, the victorious Allied nations called a conference at Bretton Woods in New Hampshire. The purpose of this Bretton Woods conference was to design a postwar international payments system. Keynes was the chief representative of the United Kingdom. In contrast to the classical view of the desirability of free exchange rate markets, at the 1944 Bretton Woods conference, Keynes's position was that there is an incompatibility thesis in the classical theory approach to international trade and finance.

Keynes argued that permitting free trade, flexible exchange rates, and free capital mobility across international borders can be incompatible with the economic goal of global full employment and rapid economic growth. Keynes offered an alternative to the classical approach to the problem. This alternative was the "Keynes Plan" solution, an arrangement that would make international trade and financial flow arrangement compatible with global full employment and vigorous economic growth while permitting nations to introduce capital controls across national boundaries.

Keynes argued that the "main cause of failure" of any traditional international payments system—whether based on fixed or flexible exchange rates—was its inability to actively foster continuous global economic expansion whenever persistent trade payment imbalances occurred among trading nations. This failure, Keynes wrote,

> can be traced to a single characteristic. I ask close attention to this, because I shall argue that this provides a clue to the nature of any alternative which is to be successful.
>
> It is characteristic of a freely convertible international standard that it throws the main burden of adjustment on the country which is the *debtor* position on the international balance of payments—that is, on the country which is (in this context) by hypothesis the *weaker* and above all the *smaller* in comparison with the other side of the scales which (for this purpose) is the rest of the world.[1]

Keynes concluded that an essential improvement in designing any international payments system requires transferring the major *onus* of adjustment from the debtor to the creditor nation. This transfer of responsibility for ending persistent trade imbalances to those nations that persistently experience exports that exceed their imports would, Keynes explained, substitute an expansionist, in place of a contractionist, pressure on world trade. To achieve a golden era of economic development, Keynes recommended combining a fixed, but adjustable, exchange rate system with a mechanism for requiring the nation "enjoying" a favorable balance of trade to initiate most of the effort necessary to eliminate this trade imbalance, while "maintaining enough discipline in the debtor countries to prevent them from exploiting the new ease allowed them."

After World War II, the war-torn capitalist nations in Europe did not have sufficient undamaged productive resources available to produce enough to feed their populations and rebuild their economies. Economic rebuilding would require the European nations to run huge import surpluses with the United States in order to meet their economic needs for recovery. The European nations had very little foreign reserves. (Foreign reserves are liquid assets that European war-devastated nations could sell for U.S. dollars, which they could then use to buy imports from the only foreign nation that had enough productivity capacity to produce for exports—the United States.)

With insufficient foreign reserves to obtain the necessary imports from the United States, the only alternative, under a free market laissez-faire system, would be for Europeans to obtain an enormous volume of loans from the United States to finance the purchase of required U.S. exports needed to feed the Europeans and rebuild their economies. Private sector lenders in the United States, however, were mindful that German reparation payments to the victorious Allied nations after World War I were primarily financed by American private investors lending to Germany (the so-called Dawes Plan). Germany never repaid these Dawes Plan loans. Given this history and existing circumstances, it was obvious that private lending facilities could not be expected to provide the credits necessary for European recovery after World War II.

The Keynes Plan, presented at the 1944 Bretton Woods conference, required the United States, as the obvious major creditor nation, to accept responsibility for solving the trade imbalance that was associated with the need of postwar European nations for U.S. imports. Keynes estimated that the United States would have to provide $10 billion to the European nations. The Keynes Plan had an operational system that would have the United States provide these funds to the Europeans. The U.S. representative to the Bretton Woods conference, Harry Dexter White, argued that Congress would never provide the $10 billion that Keynes estimated was required. Instead, White argued, Congress would be willing to provide, at most, $3 billion as the U.S. contribution to solving this postwar international financial problem.

The U.S. delegation at the Bretton Woods conference was the most important participant. It was clear that nothing could be done unless the U.S. delegation agreed to any plan that was developed at the conference. The U.S. delegation vetoed the Keynes Plan. Instead, the U.S. plan set up the International Monetary Fund (IMF) and what we now call the World Bank.

The U.S. plan envisioned the IMF providing short-term loans to nations running unfavorable balances of trade. These loans were supposed to give the debtor nation time to get its economic house in order and to stop importing more than it was exporting. The United States would subscribe a maximum of $3 billion as its contribution to the IMF lending facilities. The World Bank would borrow funds from the marketplace. These funds would then be used to provide long-term loans for rebuilding capital facilities and making capital improvements initially in the war-torn nations and later in the less developed countries. This plan was basically the institutional arrangements adopted at the Bretton Woods conference.

Under the U.S. plan, international loans from the IMF or the World Bank were the only available sources for financing the huge volume of imports from the United States that the war-torn nations would require *immediately* after World War II. The IMF and World Bank together did not have sufficient funds to make loans of the magnitude needed by the European nations. Even if they could have provided sufficient loans, European nations would have had to accept a huge international indebtedness. The European nations' electorate might opt for a communist system rather than face the huge international loan obligations that would be necessary to rebuild.

To ensure that communism did not spread west from the Soviet Union, in 1947 the United States produced the Marshall Plan, which provided $5 billion in foreign aid over 18 months and a total of $13 billion over four years. (Adjusted for inflation, this sum is equivalent to approximately $150 billion in 2008 dollars.) The recipient nations did not have any obligation to repay Marshall Plan funds. The Marshall Plan was essentially a four-year *gift* of $13 billion worth of American exports to the war-devastated nations. The Marshall Plan allowed the recipient nations to purchase U.S. exports equal to 2 percent of the total annual output of the United States for four years, from 1947 to 1951. Yet no U.S. resident felt deprived, and the Marshall Plan required no real sacrifice for American households. American household income continued to grow throughout the Marshall Plan period.

Immediately after the war ended, government military spending was significantly reduced, which by itself might have created significant postwar unemployment problems. Offsetting this reduction in military spending were the Marshall Plan funds, which the recipient nations used to purchase American exports, thereby encouraging employment increases in U.S. export industries just as several million men and women were discharged from the armed forces and entered the labor force. (Also, pent-up consumer demand from the high income earned by American workers during the war resulted in a large increase in consumer spending.) For the first time in its history, the United States did not suffer from a severe recession due to a lack of spending immediately following the cessation of a major war. Instead, the United States and most of the rest of the world experienced an economic "free lunch." Both the potential debtor nations and the creditor nation experienced tremendous real economic gains resulting from the Marshall Plan.

The moral of this Marshall Plan experience is that when the creditor nation accepts responsibility for ending a persistent trade and international payments imbalance, the result is a win-win situation for both deficit and surplus nations. This situation has obvious implications for the current international trade situation, where the United States has been running trade deficits for several decades and Japan, India, and China have relied on running export surpluses to grow their economies.

By 1958, however, although the United States still had an annual goods and services export surplus of over $5 billion, U.S. governmental foreign and military aid exceeded $6 billion, while there was a net private capital outflow of $1.6 billion. The postwar U.S. potential surplus on international payments balance was at an end as a total of $2.6 billion more funds flowed out of the United States than flowed in due to foreigners' spending on U.S. exports.

Other nations began to experience international payments surpluses. These credit-surplus nations did not spend their surpluses on additional imports from the United States. Rather, they used their dollar surpluses to purchase international liquid assets in the form of gold reserves from the U.S. Federal Reserve System. At the same time, a rebuilt Europe and Japan became important producers of exports, and the rest of the world became less dependent on the U.S. export industries.

In 1958 alone, the United States sold more than $2 billion in gold reserves to foreign central banks, while American exports to Europe declined significantly. As a result, the U.S. economy went into recession, and the economies of other countries quickly followed.

In the 1960s, trade-surplus nations continued to convert the value of their export surpluses into demands on U.S. gold reserves to be used as liquidity time machines in international markets.

The seeds of the destruction of the Bretton Woods system and the golden age of economic development were being sown as surplus nations drained U.S. gold reserves.

In 1971, President Richard Nixon declared that the U.S. government would no longer sell gold to foreign nations that had earned dollars and wanted to buy gold rather than purchase American-produced goods. In essence, the United States unilaterally withdrew from the Bretton Woods agreement. By 1971, the last vestiges of Keynes's enlightened international monetary approach, where the creditor nation accepts a large responsibility for correcting persistent trade imbalances, were forgotten.

Since then, the United States has tended to run unfavorable trade balances as other nations pursued an economic growth policy based on continual expansion of export sales to the United States—the largest market for consumer goods in the world. Export industries were the backbone propping up the economies of many nations, especially those in Asia. As long as Americans were willing to buy more imports from foreigners than what they exported to foreigners, the United States stimulated growth in these export-oriented nations.

In 2008, however, as the United States slipped into the largest economic crisis since the Great Depression, Americans dramatically reduced their spending on imports. As a result, those nations that depend on exports to drive their economies quickly slipped into recession. For example, in the fourth quarter of 2008, because of a precipitous drop in exports, the Japanese gross domestic product fell by over 12 percent.

The existing international trade and payment system permits, and actually can encourage, the spread of such depressionary forces globally. The 1944 Keynes Plan was deliberately designed to prevent the spread to other nations of a recession and failure of financial markets that might occur in any one nation. It is time to think about how we can reform the international payments system to prevent future contagion from occurring.

Reforming the International Payments System

By updating the principles underlying the Keynes Plan, it is possible to develop a twenty-first-century international monetary scheme that will promote global economic prosperity and still meet today's political realities without pandering to efficient market advocates. As Keynes wrote: "[T]o suppose [as the conventional wisdom does] that there exists some smoothly functioning automatic [free market] mechanism of adjustment which preserves equilibrium if only we trust to methods of *laissez-faire* is a doctrinaire delusion which disregards the lessons of historical experience without having behind it the support of sound theory."[2]

Since the Mexican peso crisis of 1994, some pragmatic policy makers have recognized that free markets are not sufficient to prevent periodic crises in the international payments sector. Instead, they have advocated the creation of some sort of *crisis manager* to stop international financial market liquidity hemorrhaging and to bail out international investors whenever such a crisis occurs. In 1994, after the Mexican peso crisis, Treasury Secretary Robert Rubin encouraged President Clinton to act as a crisis manager by lending American funds to Mexico and thereby to save the wealth of international buyers of Mexican bonds.

In 1997, Thailand, Malaysia, and other East Asian nations experienced an international currency crisis that battered their economies. In 1998, the Russian debt default caused another crisis that led to the collapse of the Long Term Capital Management (LTCM) hedge fund. Except for quick action by the New York Federal Reserve, that collapse could have induced a significant drop in American equity markets. (Note that among the principals of LTCM was Myron Scholes, who won a Nobel Prize for discovering the formula for "properly" pricing risk in an efficient financial market environment. Not even the Scholes formula could save LTCM from its investment blunders.)

At the time of the Russian debt default and the LTCM collapse, President Clinton called for a "new financial architecture" for international financial market transactions to prevent future international payment crises. In other words, the policy goal should be crisis prevention rather than crisis management.

IMF director Stanley Fischer also recognized that the IMF did not have sufficient funds to stem the crisis that was occurring. Fischer suggested that the major nations of the world, the so-called Group of 7 (G-7) nations, make a temporary arrangement where they would provide additional financing to help provide funds to any nations suffering from deficits in international payments until such nations could get their economic houses in order. Fischer's cry for a G-7 temporary collaboration to provide funds to deficit nations is equivalent to recruiting a volunteer fire department to douse the flames after someone has cried fire in a crowded theater. Even if the fire ultimately is extinguished, there will be a lot of innocent casualties. Moreover, every new currency fire would require the G-7 voluntary fire department to pour more liquidity into the market to put out the flames. A more desirable goal would be to produce a permanent fire prevention system and not to rely on organizing larger and larger volunteer companies with each new crisis. In other words, crisis prevention rather than crisis management should be the policy goal.

President Clinton's clarion call for a new international financial architecture implicitly recognized this need for a permanent change and improvement in the existing international payments system. Unfortunately, President Clinton's call was not taken up as the international community managed to muddle through the experience, although some nations and their residents suffered severe economic pains.

In 2007, another collapse of the international financial system began. The U.S. subprime mortgage crisis has created a contagious disease that has caused havoc with banking systems in Germany, the United Kingdom, France, Spain, and elsewhere. The contagion has caused the complete collapse of the Icelandic banking system. As these words are being written, even Swiss banking—usually considered a paragon of financial stability—is in severe economic trouble. The need for a new international financial architecture is more urgent than ever.

In the twenty-first-century interdependent global economy, a substantial degree of economic cooperation among trading nations is essential. The original Keynes Plan for reforming the international payments system called for the creation of a single supranational central bank. In recent writings,[3] I have developed a more modest proposal for a new international financial architecture. Nevertheless, my proposal would operate under the same economic principles laid down by Keynes at Bretton Woods. Rather than requiring the establishment of a supranational world central bank, my plan aims at obtaining a more modest, acceptable international agreement that does not require any nation to surrender control of either its domestic banking system or the operation of its domestic monetary and fiscal policies to a supranational authority. Each nation still will be able to determine the best economic destiny for its citizens provided this destiny does not negatively affect employment and income-earning opportunities in trading partner nations.

A closed, double-entry bookkeeping clearing institution is necessary to keep the payments "score" among the various trading nations plus some mutually agreed-on rules to solve the problems of persistent trade and payments imbalances and to prevent international financial market transactions that can disrupt the stability of a nation's economy and/or threaten the global economy.

I have called the new international institution to be set up under this plan the International Monetary Clearing Union (IMCU). All international payments, whether for imports or financial funds crossing national borders, would go through this clearing union. Each nation's central bank will set up a deposit account with the IMCU. Any payments of a resident entity in nation A made to a resident entity in nation B would have to clear through each nation's central bank deposit at the IMCU. When cleared through the IMCU, a payment from a resident in nation A to a resident in nation B would appear as a credit for nation B's central bank's account at the IMCU and as a debit to nation A's central bank's account at the IMCU. Although the process may seem complicated to laypeople, it is merely an international version of how checks are cleared when a resident of one region of the United States (say, California) pays other entities in another region (say, New York). The checks clear through the clearinghouse mechanism set up by the U.S. Federal Reserve.

This IMCU is a twenty-first-century variant of the Keynes Plan. To operate it would require at least eight technical proposals for dealing with all types of international financial problems. For the purpose of our discussion, however, I will not delve into these technical details. Instead, I will merely elaborate the principles involved in a Keynes Solution for an IMCU designed to end the possibility of persistent trade imbalances and disruptive flows of financial funds across national borders while simultaneously encouraging global full employment and economic growth.

The three objectives of this IMCU are to:

1. Prevent a lack of global effective market demand for the products of industry from occurring due to liquidity problems whenever any nation holds excessive idle reserves by saving too much of its internationally earned income. In other words, this IMCU should encourage sufficient global spending to produce enough profit incentives in export industries to help ensure global full employment.
2. Provide an automatic mechanism for placing a major burden of correcting international trade imbalances on the nation running persistent export surpluses.
3. Provide each nation with the ability to monitor and, if desired, to control movements out of the nation of:
   a. Financial funds as well as money moved across national borders in order to avoid paying taxes on such funds.
   b. Earnings from illegal activities leaving the nation.
   c. Funds that cross borders to finance terrorist operations.

For our discussion, the most important principle involved is that of items (1) and (2). The IMCU system must have a built-in mechanism that encourages any nation that runs persistent trade surpluses of exports over imports to spend what is deemed (in advance) by agreement of the international community to be "excessive" credit balances (savings) of foreign liquid reserve assets that have been deposited in the nation's deposit account at the IMCU. These accumulated credits (savings out of international earned income) represent funds that the creditor nation could have used to buy the products of foreign industries but instead used to increase its foreign reserves in terms of its deposit at the IMCU. This involves the recognition that when a nation holds excessive credits in its deposit account at the IMCU, these excess credits are creating unemployment problems and the lack of profitable opportunities for enterprises somewhere in the global economy.

If the creditor nation spends its excess credits, this spending will increase profit opportunities and the hiring of workers around the globe and thereby promote global full employment. The Keynes Solution would encourage creditor nations to spend these excess credits in three ways:

1. on the products of any other IMCU member;
2. on new direct foreign investment projects in other IMCU member nations; and/or
3. to provide foreign aid, similar to the Marshall Plan, to deficit IMCU members.

The creditor nations are free to choose any combination of these three ways to spend their excess credit at the IMCU.

Spending excessive credits on products of other IMCU members encourages the surplus nation to create profits and jobs in other nations. This means more income for people and businesses in the nations experiencing unfavorable balances of trade and who were borrowing from foreigners to buy their excess of imports over exports. In essence, spending in this way gives deficit nations the opportunity to work their way out of international debt by earning additional income by selling additional exports to their creditors.

Direct foreign investment project spending requires a nation with excess credits in its account at the IMCU to build plant and equipment in the deficit nation, thereby increasing profits, jobs, and income in the construction industries in the latter nation. If the nation receiving this direct foreign investment is a less developed country, this foreign direct investment spending helps to build the facilities to twenty-first-century standards.

Foreign aid spending provides the deficit nation with a "gift" that it can use to reduce its debt obligations and/or buy additional products from foreign producers without going further into debt.

These three spending alternatives encourage surplus nations to accept a major responsibility for correcting trade and international payments imbalances. Nevertheless, surplus countries have considerable discretion in deciding how to accept the onus of adjustment in the way they believe is in their citizens' best interests. It does not permit, however, a surplus nation to shift the burden to the deficit nation by lending the deficit nation more and therefore imposing on it additional contractual requirements for debt repayments independent of what the deficit nation can afford.

The important thing is to make sure that continual oversaving by the surplus nation in the form of international liquid reserves is not permitted to unleash depressionary economic forces on other nations and/or to build up international debts so encumbering as to impoverish the global economy of the twenty-first century.

In the event that the surplus nation does not spend or give away the credits that are deemed "excessive" within a specified time, IMCU managers would confiscate (and redistribute to debtor members) the portion of credits deemed excessive. This last resort is the equivalent of a 100 percent tax on a nation's excessive liquidity holdings. Continual excessive liquidity holdings imply continuing and excessive unemployment in one or more nations running trade deficits; therefore, if the surplus nation does not spend its excessive surplus holdings, confiscating them and providing them to debtor nations will benefit the latter. Of course, the nation with excessive credits will recognize that these credits are subject to a 100 percent tax if not spent, so it is highly unlikely that this confiscatory tax will ever have to be enforced.

Under either a fixed or flexible exchange rate system, with each nation free to decide how much it will import, some nations will, at times, experience persistent trade deficits merely because their trading partners are not living up to their means—that is, because other nations are continually saving (hoarding) a portion of their foreign export earnings rather than spending it on the products of foreign business firms. By so doing, these oversavers are creating a lack of global market demand for the products that global industries can produce.

Under this Keynes principle requiring creditor nations to spend excessive credits, deficit countries would no longer have to tighten their belts and reduce citizens' income in an attempt to reduce imports and thereby reduce their payments imbalance because others are excessively oversaving. Instead, the system would seek to remedy the payments deficit by increasing opportunities for deficit nations to sell products profitably abroad and thereby work their way out of their otherwise deteriorating debtor position.

Currently, as the global financial crisis deepens, nations will be forced to realize that attempting to tinker with the existing system by perhaps upgrading the power of the IMF and the World Bank will not solve our developing international trade and financial payments problems. For years now, the international system has been running into trouble while patches were applied in a vain attempt to end the problems. The world lost a great opportunity in 1944 when the United States vetoed the Keynes Plan at Bretton Woods. Let us hope we do not squander this opportunity again.

When the 2009 Obama recovery plan begins to revive the American economy, then the American economy may again serve as the engine of growth for the rest of the world. The resulting import excess over exports, however, will increase the U.S. international payments imbalance problem and may create an atmosphere where many fear that the status of the dollar as the most liquid safe haven foreign reserve asset will deteriorate. Such fears can only roil global financial markets and plunge the global economy into further recession.

If this were to occur, a reform of the international trade and payments system would be even more necessary. I hope the leaders of the major nations recognize the need to adopt some form of the Keynes Plan, such as the IMCU, in order to help the global economy recover and to reinstate prosperous times.

The Case for Capital Controls

Since the future is uncertain, at any moment of time some event (ephemeral or not) may occur that can make residents of a nation feel more uncertain about the prospects of their economy. Under a system of free exchange markets, those residents can remove their savings from the domestic banking system and transfer them to the banking system of another nation that they believe is a safe harbor. Funds that leave a nation in any attempt to find a safe haven elsewhere are called "flight capital." If enough people try at the same time to move their funds from the domestic economy to this presumed safe harbor, the effect is similar to a run on a bank that causes the bank to collapse.

In the case of bank runs, a policy of insuring deposits is usually sufficient to stop them. Unfortunately, a cascade of flight capital fund movements out of a nation to a safe harbor in another nation cannot be stopped by merely insuring the deposits at domestic banks. Instead, if this flight of funds is large enough, it can bring about the collapse of the domestic economy as more and more people stop buying domestically produced goods to increase their holdings of foreign liquid assets. This situation creates significant recessionary pressures on the domestic economy, thereby making it more difficult for the government to undertake economic policies to stabilize its economy and prevent it from falling into recession or depression.

Because under my proposal all movement of funds across borders must go through the nation's central bank and then on to the IMCU, nations can monitor and stop any cross-border financial fund movements merely by refusing to allow such transactions to be processed through the central bank's deposit on the IMCU's books. Each nation can institute an effective policy to limit capital fund outflows if, for any reason, its government deems the prevention of such fund outflows in the best interests of the nation's economy.

Thus, for example, as I noted in chapter 6, if such a system was in place, the U.S. government could prohibit the creation of domestic financial markets organized by investment bankers that lack a reliable market maker institution to ensure orderliness and liquidity. Under this capital control provision, the American financial services industries would not have to fear loss of profits to foreign financial services firms that did not follow Securities and Exchange Commission rules if the commission prohibited certain financial market activities by the nation's financial services firms.

Finally, all movements of funds gained from illegal activities, funds being moved from one country to another nation in order to avoid the domestic country's tax collector, or funds raised in one country that are being funneled to other countries to finance international terrorist activities must also flow through the nation's central bank to the IMCU. Consequently, each nation has the ability to monitor and stop such cross-border transactions from occurring. Clearly this is an important aspect of the IMCU plan: it permits each nation to assure its citizens that others cannot take advantage of the international trading system to avoid paying their fair share of taxes; it constrains the international financing of terrorist organizations; and it permits governments to undermine the profitability of any international illegal drug trade.

Chapter 9

MOVING TOWARD A CIVILIZED ECONOMIC SOCIETY THAT KEYNES WOULD BE PROUD OF

A civilized society should encourage its citizens to excel in all the endeavors they undertake. A civilized society, however, must also provide its citizens with the opportunities to work at things in which they have, or can develop, the skills to excel. If a thing is worth doing, it is worth doing well. A civilized society also should encourage productive members of the community to maintain a sensitivity and compassion for the needs of others and to have open and honest contractual dealings with others. All these objectives are easier to obtain in an economic system in which everyone has the opportunity to work and earn an income. In a capitalist economy, the ability to earn an honest day's income for an honest day's work creates self-esteem for the employed person and for all the members of his or her household.

During almost all of the last four decades, however, the public debate over economic policy has been dominated by the belief that if self-interested individuals are permitted to operate in a free market without government interference and regulation, and without worrying about other members of the community, the resulting free market will bring the economy to nirvana. Yet the deregulation of financial institutions while permitting self-interested mortgage originators, investment bankers, and others to provide mortgages (often with fraudulent information) to anyone who wanted to purchase a home has brought disaster to millions of innocent homeowners who can no longer afford their mortgage payments and also to the many innocent people who have lost jobs as the global economy sinks further into recession. It is hoped that our political leaders have learned from this cataclysmic experience and never again docilely submit to the free market philosophy.

In our capitalist economic system, having a productive job is an important ingredient in providing dignity for each citizen. Accordingly, one of the first objectives of a civilized capitalist economic system is to ensure that all who are willing and able to work can obtain employment in a secure and healthy environment. The preceding chapters have explained Keynes's ideas of how government can ensure that private sector employers have sufficient profit incentives to employ all workers who are actively seeking employment.

Franklin Roosevelt was the first president to recognize the power of Keynes's philosophy that government has a positive, powerful role to play as buyer of last resort to provide employment and prosperity to all its citizens. Although Roosevelt was still hampered by fears of a national debt overwhelming the nation and burdening future generations, when the war broke out, such fears were brushed aside. Spending on winning the war financed by huge government deficits proved beyond a shadow of a doubt that the government could always play an active role in guaranteeing full-employment prosperity for its entire civilian labor force.

Republican and Democratic successors to Roosevelt adopted Keynes's policy initiatives to maintain economic prosperity, even if they did not necessarily recognize that Keynes had been the first to suggest these policy prescriptions. As we have already noted, President Truman's administration produced the Marshall Plan. In this plan, the United States, the international trade surplus nation, used its wealth to solve the trade imbalance problem, thereby creating job opportunities for Americans in the export industries while helping European nations to rebuild their national economy. Truman's successor, Dwight Eisenhower, instituted one of the largest peacetime public works programs ever undertaken, building the interstate highway system. Not only did this activity create profits and jobs in construction and related industries, but it also provided the nation with a transportation system that increased the productivity of American factories by making it less expensive to take delivery of raw materials at the factory door and less expensive to deliver the finished product to the marketplace. Such active government policies made the United States and most of the free world a more prosperous and civilized place in which to live.

Meanwhile, during these years, the Federal Reserve recognized that its primary function was to maintain the liquidity and stability of financial markets. At the same time, the Glass-Steagall Act was strictly enforced so that the banking function of making loans to customers was strictly separated from the underwriting function of investment bankers to float securities in well-organized and orderly financial markets.

With the advent of stagflation in the 1970s and the victory of Milton Friedman's free market philosophy, central banks and governments adopted a different, less civilized philosophical approach to the economy. In 1979, for example, after a second spike in crude oil prices engineered by the Organization of Petroleum Exporting Countries (OPEC), the Fed, under Chairman Paul Volker, raised interest rates to double-digit levels to deliberately destroy profit opportunities for many businesses and to create the highest unemployment rate since the Great Depression. As the U.S. economy tumbled downward and the economies of the rest of the free world also collapsed, there was a severe drop in the demand for gasoline and other petroleum products. Simultaneously, new non-OPEC crude oil supplies were coming onto the markets from regions such as the North Sea and Alaska. In the face of these challenges, the OPEC cartel could not continue to exert as much pressure on the market. Oil prices dropped and remained low for many years. The threat of a commodity inflation inducing incomes inflation as workers demanded cost-of-living increases and businesses raised prices to protect their profit margins from inflation seemed to be tamed.

The lesson taken from this 1979–1981 Fed-induced episode of a deliberate policy to create high unemployment to end a period of incomes inflation was simple, and it fit the free market philosophy. An independent central bank board of governors, whose members were not subject to political elections every two years, could make policies that the public would have to accept. These policies would be aimed at constraining inflationary forces that are unleashed when the economy becomes so prosperous that workers and managers believe that, in a free market, they can raise wages and prices without losing customers.

Instead, policy would be designed so that if inflation was larger than the central bankers felt desirable, the central bank would institute an unpopular tight money policy deliberately aimed at producing fewer profit opportunities for business firms in order to induce employers to lay off workers. Andrew Mellon's philosophical message to President Hoover was back in the corridors of power. Purging the rottenness out of the system required liquidating income-earning opportunities of businesses and workers. With loss of income opportunities, enterprises and workers will work harder and demand less when a job opportunity or profit opportunity does appear. Surely this is not a civilized solution to the economic problems of a twenty-first-century capitalist system.

Keynes's solution was simple and certainly more civilized. As long as people want to work, the government must make sure that they have an opportunity to obtain a job that fits their skills. If there is sufficient demand from private sector buyers to create market demand for all the goods and services that the nation's business firms can produce with a fully employed labor force, then the government's only responsibility is to make sure that employers are obeying the laws that a civilized society enacts to ensure safe working conditions, product safety requirements, and the like.

If, and only if, there is a significant shortfall in private sector market demand for products of the nation's industries, then the government should take an active role in pumping up demand to create profit opportunities for businesses and job opportunities for the unemployed. When a significantly large recession appears on the economic horizon and private sector buyers are reluctant to spend more of their income, the government must step in to act as the purchaser of last resort. What things should the government buy?

Keynes argued that the government should, in this case, attempt to invest in those areas that provide productivity-enhancing activities for the nation. According to Keynes, if government spending appears to be "the only means of securing an approximation to full employment...this need not exclude all manner of compromises and devices by which the public authority will co-operate with public initiative."[1]

Accordingly, productive investments include government paying private enterprises to rebuild the economic infrastructure by repairing the nation's highways, bridges, airports, and harbors. This does not mean that the government should finance the building of a "bridge to nowhere" merely to create profits and jobs—although building a bridge to nowhere is better than doing nothing. Statistics, however, indicate that in America, many bridges and highways with important destinations are urgently in need of repair.

Other infrastructure projects that would contribute to improving the health and therefore the productive life of the nation's citizens include repairing and improving the water supply system and sanitary facilities of all kinds.

If the nation and the global economy recover from the current economic crisis, then the OPEC cartel's power to raise oil prices will be enhanced. Government spending to encourage university and private sector research and development for methods to reduce the costs of delivering alternative energy sources is an obvious productive investment that will reduce the nation's dependence on oil. Upgrading the nation's electric grid also falls into the category of productive investments that will wean the economy from its overuse of the products of crude oil. Similarly, the government should encourage the development of light rail transportation systems to promote switching commuter traffic from using gasoline-consuming automobiles on our highways to efficient and reliable public transportation. Such projects also will contribute to the nation's effort to prevent global warming and reduce the atmospheric pollution that we leave to our children and grandchildren.

In our high-tech twenty-first-century global economy, education is an especially important investment project for developing the skills, knowledge, and pleasures of future generations. Local governments, which are incurring significant shortfalls in their tax receipts due to the collapsing economy, find it difficult, if not impossible, to maintain the current educational system, much less upgrade it. If the federal government would provide funding for local and state educational systems, our public schools, public community colleges, and public universities could become the platform for launching our citizens into more productive and enjoyable lives.

If, however, as Keynes warned in *The General Theory*, "we are so sensible, having schooled ourselves to so close a semblance of prudent financiers taking careful thought before we add to the 'financial' burdens of prosperity by building them houses to live in, that we have no such easy escape from the sufferings of unemployment."[2] There are those who argue that the government should not borrow to create jobs and productive investments for future generations to use, because the borrowing will burden those generations with a large national debt. They do not realize how much we will impoverish future generations by not providing these productive outcomes if the government does nothing in order to pass on a smaller national debt to posterity.

Clearly, the list of possible investment projects that government can encourage with a significant spending recovery plan is enormous. Many of these projects would be desirable to invest in even if the economy were not in a significant recession. The advantages of improving citizens' productivity are too obvious to ignore because we fear that the resulting national debt will be too burdensome for our children.

Probably an important, but potentially politically controversial, project involves investing in healthcare for all the citizens of the nation. Unlike most developed nations, the United States does not have a national program to protect the health of all its citizens. Instead, we rely on a patchwork of various health insurance programs. Since World War II, most employed workers have been covered by private health insurance plans financed primarily by their employers. These plans add significantly to a business's costs of producing and selling products. For the Big Three U.S. automakers, the cost of healthcare for employees and retirees (whose healthcare costs are also covered) per automobile produced is greater than the cost of the steel used. This fact clearly puts U.S. employers at a tremendous competitive cost disadvantage relative to foreign producers, especially in an era when free international trade is being foisted on the public.

All other retired workers who are over 65 years of age are covered by the government's Medicare health plan. For households whose workers are not covered by employee health insurance plans and for those who are unemployed for any length of time, the only way to obtain healthcare coverage is to purchase private health insurance, which often costs $1,000 per month or more. Statistics indicate that millions of Americans lack any health plan coverage and therefore do not go to doctors for preventive medicine. In the extreme, this situation results in the uninsured seeking care only after their health deteriorates significantly. Then they must throw themselves at the mercy of the hospital and/or the community to pay for their care.

It should be obvious that to participate and flourish in our economic system, access to healthcare is an urgent priority. Good health increases longevity. As Stephen P. Dunn, a senior strategy advisor to the English Department of Health and Director of Provider Development of the National Health Service East of England, states: "Reduction in avoidable disease and increases in the years of healthy life expectancy would accelerate economic growth.... The economic loss to society of shortened lives due to early death and chronic disability is hundreds of billions of dollars per year."[3]

An important question for a civilized society to decide is whether healthcare is a basic right for every member of the community. If every person is going to contribute effectively to the productive activities of the nation, and if this contribution is to be done well, then individuals and their family members must be as healthy as the practice and technological advances of medicine permit. If a civilized society recognizes the basic right of all its members to find employment where they can use their talents to turn out the best possible product, surely it can be argued that access to healthcare, paid for by the community at large, is also a basic right for each member of society. Healthier workers are always more productive workers. Keynes, who died before England instituted its national health program, does not have a facile solution to the question of whether all members of society are entitled to healthcare independent of their income. But surely some evidence indicates that access to universal healthcare independent of a family's income would be a productive investment for society to undertake.

In sum, government can finance many investment projects to encourage the private sector to produce results. The problem is not a shortage of financing; the problem is a shortage of resolve.

I hope that I have demonstrated that government regulators have an important role to play in assuring members of our society that public financial markets are well organized and orderly. Doing this will protect households that are searching for financial assets in which to place their savings in order to meet any future spending needs (anticipated or not) during their active income-earning period as well as to provide sufficient liquid purchasing power in their retirement years.

Putting the Keynes Solution into practice will not be easy. However, the solution offers more hope for a stable, prosperous economic system than does the efficient market theory that has been promoted recently, a philosophy that has brought the global economy to the brink of economic disaster.

Chapter 10

WHO WAS JOHN MAYNARD KEYNES?

A Brief Biography

John Maynard Keynes was born on June 5, 1883, the first of three children of John Neville Keynes, a Cambridge University don who taught economics, and Florence Ada Keynes. The Keynes family, residing at 6 Harvey Road in Cambridge, England, lived in moderate circumstances but solid comfort. Their house was well staffed with domestic servants. The family embodied the values of Victorian days that assumed peace, prosperity, and progress to be normal.

While John Maynard Keynes was growing up, visitors at the family residence included some of the most famous economists and philosophers of the day, including Bertrand Russell, Ludwig Wittgenstein, and Alfred Marshall. The learned discussions that must have occurred at 6 Harvey Road during Keynes's childhood and adolescence surely had an impact on his developing mind.

In 1897, at the age of 14, Keynes won a scholarship to Eton, arguably Britain's best school. Keynes was an outstanding student who excelled in mathematics, classics, and history. In 1902, Keynes was enrolled as an undergraduate student at King's College, Cambridge. There he came under the influence of the philosopher G. E. Moore, whose *Principia Ethica* (1903) became a "manifesto of modernism" to Keynes and his generation of intellectuals. At Cambridge, his best friends, including Lytton Strachey and Leonard Woolf, would become members of what was later called the Bloomsbury Group, composed of artists and intellectuals such as Virginia Woolf, Vanessa Bell, and Duncan Grant.

Upon graduation from Cambridge in 1906, Keynes scored second on the civil service exam. In a letter dated October 4, 1906, to Strachey, Keynes noted that in this exam "real knowledge seems an absolute bar to success. I have done worst in the only two subjects of which I possessed a solid knowledge, Mathematics and Economics.... For Economics I got a relatively low percentage and was 8th or 9th in order of merit—whereas I knew the *whole* of both…in a real elaborate way."[1] Later on Keynes explained his poor performance in economics by saying, "I evidently knew more about economics than my examiners."[2]

His ranking on the civil service exam permitted Keynes to accept a position as a clerk in the India Office in London. In the short time that Keynes worked there, he learned how a government office operates and developed an interest in Indian affairs and especially in the Indian monetary system. This experience would have a profound effect on his later professional work and his development of a serious economic theory regarding the role of money in the economy.

While at the India Office, Keynes worked in his spare time on the theory of probability, a subject he had written about initially in his fellowship thesis at Cambridge. He would continue for almost 15 years to spend his spare time on this subject. Finally, in 1921, he published his *Treatise on Probability*. Keynes's view on probability would later permit him to differentiate his theoretical approach to the concept of uncertainty from probabilistic risk, which was part of the theory of other leading classical economists of his time as well as of current-day efficient market theory advocates.

On his twenty-fifth birthday, Keynes resigned from the India Office to take a special lecturer position at Cambridge University. This lectureship was privately financed by A. C. Pigou, the successor to Alfred Marshall as the professor of economics at Cambridge. At Cambridge, in the years before World War I, Keynes lectured on the topic of money, credit, and prices.

With the outbreak of World War I, Keynes, unlike many of his pacifist friends from Cambridge, thought it was his duty to assist the war effort. In the September 1914 issue of the *Economic Journal*, Keynes, the editor, published a masterful article titled "War and the Financial System, August 1914." Although this article made quite a stir in the British government, Keynes did not get a government job until January 1915, when he was made an assistant to Sir George Paish, the Special Advisor to the Chancellor of the Exchequer, Lloyd George. With a change of government in May 1915, Reginald McKenna became the Chancellor of the Exchequer, and Keynes was appointed to the Treasury's No. 1 Division—the section centrally concerned with the financial direction of the war.

Keynes's work at the Treasury during World War I educated him on the importance of controlling expectations if one wanted to affect the exchange rate. At the outbreak of World War II, Keynes noted the importance of maintaining a stable exchange rate when he wrote about his experience at the Treasury during the first war. This early experience had a strong effect on Keynes's vision for the post–World War II international payments system and the need for stable exchange rates.

Roy Harrod has recorded an amusing incident in his biography of Keynes. It illustrates why Keynes's experience during World

War I led him to recognize the flimsy basis of market price asset valuation in financial markets. During that war, the English were in dire need of Spanish pesetas to purchase war-related imports from Spain. With great difficulty, Keynes managed to obtain a small amount of pesetas and duly reported this to a relieved Secretary of the Treasury, who remarked that at any rate, for a short time, they had a supply of pesetas. "Oh no!" Keynes exclaimed. "What!" said his horrified chief. Keynes responded, "I've sold them again: I'm going to break the market." And Keynes did.

For most of World War I, Keynes's primary responsibility at the Treasury was to try to manage the crisis in obtaining external finance for the many military and civilian imports that Britain needed. This experience was to put him in good stead when, during World War II, he headed the British delegation to the Bretton Woods conference on developing a postwar international payments system.

In January 1916, the British government introduced military conscription. Most of Keynes's Bloomsbury friends became conscientious objectors. Keynes argued that since Britain was already immersed in the war, it was essential to work to establish world affairs on a new and better basis so that the terrible bloodshed would never happen again. Keynes believed that he should do all that he could from his office in the Treasury to secure a durable peace and a new pattern of international relations.

As a member of the British government team at the Versailles Treaty meetings that ended World War I, Keynes was completely disheartened by a section in the treaty that imposed harsh economic penalties on the losing German nation. The Armistice of November 1918 contained a provision, inserted by the French and the British, requiring the Germans to pay "for all damage" done to the civilian population of Britain and France and to their property. Unfortunately, as Keynes recognized, the size of the postwar reparations imposed would overwhelm the German economy.

Keynes believed that the magnitude of reparations that the Allies demanded was intolerable.

After the Treaty of Versailles was signed, Keynes resigned his position at the Treasury. He wrote to the prime minister: "I am slipping away from the scene of nightmare. I can do no more good here. I've gone on hoping even through these last dreadful weeks that you'd find some way to make the Treaty a just and expedient document. But now it's apparently too late. The battle is lost."[3]

During the summer and early fall of 1919, Keynes wrote *The Economic Consequences of the Peace* to explain his disillusionment with the process that produced the Versailles peace treaty. In this book, published in December 1919, Keynes condemned the victorious Allied government leaders for the terms they demanded from Germany.

Although the book was an explanation of the reparations problem, it was not written as a technical treatise. Another Keynes biographer, Lord Robert Skidelsky, has written of this book:

> The writing is angry, scornful, and, rarely for Keynes, passionate: never again were his denunciations of bungling and lying, or his moral indignation, to ring so loud and clear.... The result is a personal statement unique in twentieth century literature. Keynes was staking the claim of the economist to be Prince. All other forms of rule were bankrupt. The economist's vision of welfare, conjoined to a new standard of technical excellence, were to be the last barriers to chaos, madness and retrogression.[4]

By August 1920, over 100,000 copies of *Economic Consequences* had been sold in Britain and America, and the book had been translated into German, Dutch, Flemish, Danish, Swedish, Italian, Spanish, Romanian, Russian, Japanese, and Chinese. With such large book sales, Keynes gained worldwide public attention and realized that he could channel his creative abilities into making the economic system a haven for creative artists. Keynes seized this opportunity to assert not only his own claim for attention but also the claim of economic science to shape the future.

Between 1922 and 1936, the unemployment rate in Britain fell below 10 percent only once: in 1927, when it was 9.7 percent. This long period of unemployment distress in Britain seemed to destroy all hope for advancing a civilized society. The British economic experience of the 1920s made it obvious to Keynes that orthodox classical theory could not provide the guidelines to create a civilized capitalist system. With the unemployment rate stuck near or above 10 percent for almost 14 years, it was apparent that the classical theory argument that free markets would ensure full employment was not applicable to the world of experience. To a man of Keynes's creative abilities, it became obvious that what was necessary was a new economic theory to provide an understanding of an economic system that could perpetuate widespread unemployment. Intelligent application of this new theory would once again set humankind along the path to a more civilized society. The path to creating this new economic theory would be a long and arduous one. It would take Keynes more than a decade to develop his revolutionary ideas.

After World War I, Keynes returned to teaching at Cambridge University. Keynes, however, was not an ivory tower academic economist. Besides his teaching position as bursar of Kings College, Keynes made important investment decisions involving the college's large portfolio of investments. He also served on the boards of several insurance and investment companies and in so doing obtained firsthand knowledge of participants' behavior in financial markets. Moreover, his experience as a civil servant in the India Office, as well as his service in the Treasury, enabled Keynes to recognize the need to convert theoretical prescriptions into politically acceptable, workable plans. Keynes was truly an economist of the real world.

On August 4, 1925, Keynes married Lydia Lopokova, a famous Russian ballerina. They had no children.

Although Keynes was often quoted in newspapers regarding the economic problems of the day, he did not have another position in the British government until the outbreak of World War II, at which time he was given an office but no official position. He was free to float from economic problem to economic problem and provide advice to government officials. In 1942, Keynes was made a baron and could sit in the House of Lords in the English Parliament. In 1944, he was appointed to be the head of the British delegation to the Bretton Woods conference, which was held to establish the postwar international payments system.

Keynes died on April 21, 1946, at the age of 62.

APPENDIX

Why Keynes's Ideas Were Never Taught in American Universities

A sage once defined a "classic" as "a book everyone cites but no one reads." For textbook writers and economics professors, Keynes's 1936 book, *The General Theory of Employment, Interest and Money*, is, therefore, truly a classic.

For several decades after World War II, economists spoke about a Keynesian revolution in economic theory and policy. What these economists who labeled themselves devout followers of the Keynesian revolution discussed, however, had no connection to Keynes's analysis of the operation of a money-using, market-oriented capitalist economy. As this appendix demonstrates, economics professors at our most prestigious universities or the author of the bestselling "Keynesian" textbook never understood Keynes's analytical framework.

This charade of passing off an analysis that had nothing to do with Keynes as "Keynesian" went on until the 1970s. Then the problem of inflation induced by the price spike in oil produced by the Organization of Petroleum Exporting Countries (OPEC) revealed that the prominent Keynesians of the time, who had no knowledge of Keynes's analysis of commodity inflation or incomes inflation, could not provide a cogent policy to fight the inflation. Free market advocates found these Keynesians easy targets and destroyed what was passing as their Keynesian policy arguments. In academia, the victory of the free marketers was so complete that students were taught to believe that the classical efficient market theorists had buried forever Keynes's critique of the faults of a capitalist economy and the necessity for government to play an active role in overcoming these faults.

The apparent resurrection and deification of classical theory in the 1970s was, in fact, not a rising of the theory from the dead. Established leaders and trendsetters of the economics profession never understood Keynes's analysis. Almost as soon as Keynes published his revolutionary monetary theory, it was aborted for two reasons. First, mainstream professors of economics believed that Keynes's explanation of unemployment required wage and price rigidities rather than an analysis that placed the unemployment problem in the context of desire for liquidity and the functioning of financial markets. Second, the anticommunist atmosphere (McCarthyism) rampant in the United States in the years immediately after World War II discouraged any teaching of Keynes's true message.

Why Keynes's Book Is an Economic Classic

The failure of his analysis to revolutionize the way mainstream economists build theories to explain the real world ultimately would not have surprised Keynes. In his inaugural lecture before the British Academy on April 22, 1971, the Cambridge economist Austin Robinson, quoting from an unpublished early draft of Keynes's *General Theory*, stated that Keynes wrote: " 'In economics you cannot *convict* your opponent of error, you can only *convince* him of it. And even if you are right, you cannot convince him...if his head is already filled with contrary notions that he cannot catch the clues to your thought which you are throwing to him.'"

Not only Keynes's generation of economic theorists, but also, as this chapter demonstrates, younger post–World War II economists such as Nobel Prize winners Milton Friedman and Paul Samuelson had their heads so full of the contrary notions of classical theory that they could not catch the thoughts that Keynes was throwing to all who would listen.

Keynes's biographer Lord Robert Skidelsky has stated that "mainstream economists after the Second World War treated Keynes's theory as a 'special case' of the classical theory, applicable to conditions where money wages...were 'sticky' [i.e., very slow to change or rigid]. Thus his theory was robbed of its theoretical bite, while allowed to retain its relevance for policy."[1]

If Keynes was merely arguing that unemployment was the result of price and wage rigidities, then he was not providing a revolutionary theoretical analysis of the major economic problem of a money-using capitalist economy, namely the failure to provide a persistent full-employment environment. Nineteenth-century economists had argued already that the lack of freely flexible wages and prices (what modern mainstream economists call supply side imperfections) were the sole cause of unemployment.

In chapter 19 of his *General Theory*, Keynes specifically stated that his theory of unemployment did not rely on the assumption of wage and/or price rigidities. He claimed that his theory provided a different analysis where the cause of unemployment was related to the operation of financial markets and the public's desire to hold liquid assets. After World War II, however, university economics students were taught that the Keynesian revolution required the assumption of sticky wages and/or prices to explain the existence of involuntary unemployment. Obviously the professors believed *The General Theory* was a classic since they apparently never read chapter 19, even though they cited the book as the masterpiece of Keynes's analysis.

The fact that eminent professors either did not read or did not understand Keynes's book is clear from the following incident. In 1972, I and several others had a printed debate with Milton Friedman that was published in the *Journal of Political Economy*. (In 1974, this debate was republished as a book entitled *Milton Friedman's Monetary Framework: A Debate with His Critics*.) In that debate, I pointed out to Friedman that in chapter 19, page 257, of *The General Theory*, Keynes specifically stated that his analysis did not rely on any rigidity of money wages or prices. Friedman's response, on pages 148–49 of the debate book, was that "the four chapters Davidson refers to contains many correct, interesting and valuable ideas although also some wrong ones....But all four chapters are strictly peripheral to the main contribution of the *General Theory*." Instead, on page 44 of this debate book, Friedman insisted, without providing any citations, that "[t]he rigid price assumption of Keynes...is entirely a *deus ex machina* with no underpinning in economic theory." By accusing Keynes of making an assumption that Keynes never made, Friedman enabled himself and his followers to dismiss Keynes as developing a theory without any underpinnings.

In the immediate postwar period, some professors attempted to bolster this wage and price rigidity argument by adding, as an additional cause of unemployment equilibrium, the existence of an interest rate stickiness, or fixity. This fixed interest rate argument was called the "liquidity trap," and the concept sometimes is still used today by the media to explain why the economy cannot get out of a recession. This liquidity trap is said to occur where at some low, but positive, rate of interest, the demand to hold money is assumed to be unlimited and no one will hold any debt instruments in his or her portfolio. Thus, according to liquidity trap theorists, interest rates cannot decline further and monetary policy cannot induce any further increases in investment expenditures necessary to expand the economy toward a full-employment outcome. After World War II, however, econometric studies could not find any evidence of the existence of a liquidity trap in the historical data.

Had mainstream economists read *The General Theory*, however, they would have known that on page 202 Keynes specified that the demand for money can never become unlimited at some positive rate of interest. Moreover, eyeballing historical data led Keynes to state, on page 207, that he knew of no historical example where the liquidity preference function became "virtually absolute." In sum, from both a theoretical and an empirical view, Keynes had already denied the existence of a liquidity trap. This liquidity trap conceptual apparatus has no relationship to Keynes's argument, although people calling themselves Keynesians often trot it out in public discussion.

From these illustrations, it should be obvious that most postwar economists either never read or never understood Keynes's book. In fact, in most prestigious universities, economics department students have been taught that *The General Theory of Employment, Interest and Money* is an obscure and confusing book and therefore they need not read or comprehend it. For example, N. Greg Mankiw, a self-proclaimed New Keynesian economist, a Harvard University professor, and a former chairman of President George W. Bush's Council of Economic Advisors, has written that the "*General Theory* is an obscure book....[It] is an outdated book....We are in a much better position than Keynes was to figure out how the economy works....Few macro economists take such a dim view of classical economics [as Keynes did]....Classical economics is right in the long run. Moreover, economists today are more interested in the long-run equilibrium....[There is] widespread acceptance of classical economics."[2]

When distinguished professors say such things, it is obvious that students of economics will neither read nor try to comprehend Keynes's "obscure" message. Instead, these students are told that the "Keynesian" argument boils down to the classical theory view that the basic causes of observed unemployment in the world are primarily supply side imperfections, especially due to the rigidity of money wages in the labor market of the last half century, where the "welfare" state has coddled workers by legislating minimum wages, encouraging labor union organization, and providing "lavish" unemployment benefits.

Consequently, it should not be surprising that graduates of distinguished economics departments who are advisors to government policymakers suggest that if nations are to fight the persistent levels of unemployment that plague many developed nations in today's globalized economy, labor markets must be "liberalized." Labor markets must be completely deregulated, and the social safety net that prevents unemployment from being an unmitigated disaster for workers must be reduced, if not completely removed.

If labor market "liberalization" is taken to its theoretical extreme, there would be no government rules regarding minimum workshop safety conditions or even the prohibition of child labor. The Chinese labor market would, therefore, be the ideal that other nations should attempt to emulate. To possess such an ideal global labor market, Western nations should dismantle any existing social safety net until their labor market conditions are comparable to those in the less developed nations.

How "Keynesianism" Migrated to American Textbooks

To explain why Keynes's revolutionary claim that the explanation of unemployment was nested in the desire of people to use liquid assets as a store of value never had a chance of becoming the foundation of economic analysis, I focus primarily on the example of Paul Samuelson's attempt to propagate Keynesianism via a post–World War II textbook.

Most students who studied economics during the last half of the twentieth century thought of Samuelson as a disciple of Keynes and his revolutionary general theory analysis. Samuelson is usually considered the founder of the American Keynesian school, which he called neoclassical synthesis Keynesianism because of the classical economic theory that Samuelson believed was the foundation of Keynes's economic analysis.

Samuelson's Ph.D. thesis won the Wells Prize (an annual award for the best doctoral dissertation in economics at Harvard) and was published in 1947 under the title *Foundations of Economic Analysis*. In this volume, Samuelson spelled out in precise mathematical terms the basis of early twentieth-century classical economic theory (then often called "neoclassical theory"). Accordingly, it should not be surprising that, in the 1940s, Samuelson used his dissertation presentation of neoclassical theory as the foundation for his brand of Keynesianism. Unfortunately, his neoclassical synthesis Keynesianism is not logically compatible with the theoretical framework developed by Keynes in *The General Theory of Employment, Interest and Money*. As I have already noted in chapter 4, as late as 1969, Samuelson was asserting that the ergodic axiom was an essential element if economics was to be a true "science." This assertion alone should be sufficient to suggest that the founder of the American school of Keynesianism did not understand what Keynes's revolution was about, since one of the fundamental classical axioms that Keynes discarded in building his theory was the ergodic axiom.

Moreover, there is important additional evidence to explain why Samuelson's Keynesianism was not what Keynes's analysis was about and why no one in academia in the 1940s or 1950s challenged Samuelson.

In their wonderful 1996 book *The Coming of Keynesianism to America*, David Colander and Harry Landreth credit Samuelson with saving the textbook pedagogical basis of the Keynesian revolution from destruction by the anticommunist spirit (McCarthyism) that ravaged American academia and politics in the years immediately following World War II.

Lorie Tarshis, a Canadian who had attended Keynes's lectures at Cambridge during the early 1930s, published in 1947 *The Elements of Economics* (Houghton Mifflin, Norton), an introductory economics textbook that incorporated his lecture notes interpretation of Keynes's *General Theory*. Colander and Landreth indicate that despite the initial popularity of Tarshis's book, its sales declined rapidly as trustees of, and donors to, American colleges and universities attacked it as preaching economic heresy. The frenzy about Tarshis's textbook reached a pinnacle when William F. Buckley, in his 1951 book *God and Man at Yale*, devoted a chapter to attacking the Tarshis textbook that was in use at Yale as communist inspired.

In an August 1986 interview, Colander and Landreth asked Paul Samuelson about his becoming an economist and a "Keynesian." Samuelson responded that he had recognized the "virulence of the attack on Tarshis" and so he wrote his textbook, *Principles of Economics*, "carefully and lawyer like," and, when Tarshis's textbook was attacked, Samuelson began calling his analysis neoclassical synthesis Keynesianism. It would appear that Samuelson's assertion and belief that his brand of Keynesian economics is synthesized with (and based on) traditional classical economic theory assumptions made his version of Keynesianism less open to attacks of bringing economic heresy into university courses on economics. Samuelson was claiming that the basis of his version of Keynesianism was orthodox neoclassical theory that claimed free markets assured full employment as long as prices and wages were flexible. Hence it was the rigidity or fixity of wages that was the cause of unemployment. This rigidity of money wages could always be blamed on labor unions and/or government setting a minimum wage.

Samuelson's Keynesianism also was embedded in some simple mathematical equations that he claimed captured Keynes's entire argument. This mathematical derivation plus its claimed synthesis of neoclassical theory made it more difficult to attack the Samuelson version of textbook Keynesianism as politically motivated. Thus, for several generations of economists educated after World War II, Samuelson's name was synonymous with Keynesian theory. Various editions of Samuelson's textbook were best sellers for almost a half century. Even those younger economists who ultimately broke with the old neoclassical synthesis Keynesianism and developed their own brand of "New Keynesianism" based their analytical approach on Samuelson's *Foundation of Economic Analysis* and its classical economic axiomatic foundations.

From a historical perspective, it appears that Samuelson may have saved the textbook pedagogical basis of the Keynesian revolution from destruction by McCarthyism simply by ignoring the less restrictive axiomatic foundation of Keynes's analytic revolution. But the question remains: Did Samuelson really understand Keynes's analysis and just use the neoclassical framework to protect his book from political attack?

In his 1986 interview, Samuelson indicated that in the period before World War II, his "friends who were not economists regarded [him] as very conservative." Samuelson graduated from the University of Chicago in June 1935. Had he not received a Social Science Research Council fellowship upon graduation, which sent him to Harvard, he would have done his graduate studies at the University of Chicago and probably would have been a classmate of Milton Friedman. What information about Keynes's *General Theory*, published in 1936, was Samuelson exposed to at Harvard?

Robert Bryce, a Canadian, had attended Keynes's Cambridge lectures between the fall of 1932 and the spring of 1935. In a 1987 interview with Colander and Landreth, Bryce indicated that in the spring of 1935, he spent half of each week at the London School of Economics (LSE) and half at Cambridge University. At LSE, Bryce used his notes taken during Keynes's lectures to write an essay on Keynes's revolutionary ideas—without even having read *The General Theory*. Bryce's essay so impressed LSE professor Frederick Hayek, a world-famous classical theorist, that Hayek let Bryce explain Keynes's ideas, as Bryce had written them out in this essay, during four consecutive weeks of Hayek's LSE seminar. Bryce's LSE presentations were a huge success.

In the fall of 1935, Bryce went to Harvard, where he stayed for two years. Beginning in the winter of 1936, an informal group met during the evenings to discuss Keynes's book. Bryce, using the same pre–*General Theory* essay that had been the basis for his talks at LSE, presented what he believed was Keynes's analysis—although he still had not read the *General Theory*. In 1936, Bryce's essay became the basis of what most economists at Harvard, probably including Samuelson, thought was Keynes's analysis—even though Bryce had not read the book when he wrote his essay explaining what Keynes's theory was and made his presentations at LSE and Harvard. Even in 1987, Bryce stated that "anyone who studies that book is going to get very confused. It was...a difficult, provocative book."

The immediate question therefore is: Did Bryce ever really comprehend the basis of Keynes's analytical framework? And if he did not, how did that affect how the young Samuelson and others at Harvard in 1936 learning about Keynes's analytical framework? Bryce's presentations at LSE and Harvard were supposed to make Keynes's ideas readily understandable—something that Bryce believed Keynes did not do in his *General Theory* book.

Samuelson told Colander and Landreth that he gained his first knowledge of Keynes's *General Theory* from Bryce. More important, even after reading *The General Theory* in 1936, Samuelson stated that he found its analysis "unpalatable" and not comprehensible. In his interview with Colander and Landreth, Samuelson said: "The way I finally convinced myself was to just stop worrying about it [about understanding Keynes's analysis]. I asked myself: why do I refuse a paradigm that enables me to understand the Roosevelt upturn from 1933 till 1937?...I was content to assume that there was enough rigidity in relative prices and wages to make the Keynesian alternative to Walras operative."[3] In other words, *Samuelson admits he did not understand Keynes's analysis. Instead, he assumed that Keynes was presenting a traditional general equilibrium classical theory model where wage and price rigidity caused unemployment.*

This direct quote from Samuelson should make it apparent that his mind was already so filled with contrary classical theory notions that he never made any attempt to understand Keynes's general theory analytical foundation, which rested on removing three classical axioms. In 1986, 50 years after Keynes's *General Theory* was published, Samuelson was still claiming that "we [Keynesians] always assumed that the Keynesian underemployment equilibrium floated on a substructure of administered prices and imperfect competition." When pushed by Colander and Landreth regarding whether this requirement of wage and price rigidity was ever formalized in his work, Samuelson's response was: "There was no need to." If sticky wages and prices cause unemployment, however, there was nothing revolutionary about Keynes's analysis. After all, nineteenth-century economists had already demonstrated that if wages were rigid in a Walrasian classical theory model, unemployment would result.

At the same time that Samuelson became a Keynesian by convincing himself not to worry about Keynes's actual analytical framework, Tarshis had obtained a position at Tufts University, a mere half hour away from Harvard. Tarshis often met with the group at Harvard, including Bryce, who were discussing Keynes. In his interview with Colander and Landreth, Tarshis states: "Paul Samuelson was not in the Keynesian group. He was busy working on his own thing. That he became a Keynesian is laughable."

Yet Paul Samuelson has called himself a "Keynesian" and even a "post-Keynesian" in several editions of his famous textbook. Nevertheless, it should be obvious that by his own admission Samuelson, who became the premier American Keynesian of his time, had not understood Keynes's *General Theory* book.

Given Samuelson's dominance of the global economics profession after World War II, Samuelson's neoclassical theory became the foundation of what professors and students of economics believed was Keynes's theory. Accordingly, Keynes's revolutionary

General Theory analysis was never adopted as part of mainstream economics. Consequently, in the 1970s academic literature, true classical economists, such as the monetarist school leader Milton Friedman of the University of Chicago, easily defeated Samuelson's "Keynesianism" on the grounds of the logical inconsistencies between Samuelson's neoclassical foundations and his "Keynesian" economic policy prescriptions.

This victory of classical theory over Samuelson's brand of Keynesianism changed the domestic and international choices of economic policies deemed socially acceptable by politicians and their economic advisors to prevent unemployment, to promote economic development, and even to finance government Social Security systems away from prescriptions compatible with Keynes's *General Theory* and toward the age-old, laissez-faire free market policies advocated by the classical theory that had dominated nineteenth- and early-twentieth-century thought. Prior to Friedman's classical theory victory, postwar governments, whether liberal or conservative, actively pursued the types of economic policies Keynes had advocated in the 1930s and 1940s (even though Keynesian professors and their students who became political advisors had little knowledge of Keynes's actual analysis).

In the 1980s, a new brand of Keynesianism called "New Keynesian theory" was developed and replaced Samuelson's neoclassical Keynesianism. Just as Friedman's arguments had conquered Samuelson's brand of Keynesianism by exploiting the latter's logical inconsistencies, the 1980s version of classical theory—called new classical theory, based on the rational expectations hypothesis of Nobel Prize winner Robert Lucas—easily made a mockery of the New Keynesian approach, which still relied on the rigidity of wages and prices to explain unemployment.

Rational expectations require the ergodic axiom as a logical foundation and therefore presumed that with free markets, there already existed a long-run full-employment economic future that could not be altered by human actions and government policies.

Accordingly, the new classicists could argue that our economic problems were associated with short-run supply side problems, primarily due to government interference with competition in the labor and product marketplace. If markets could be freed from government interference, new classical theorists could demonstrate that even in the short run, the economy could achieve full-employment prosperity. If these government restrictions were not removed, then it might take until the long run, as Mankiw noted in a quotation cited earlier, until the classical theory provided the right conclusions. The result of the classical victory over both neoclassical synthesis Keynesians and New Keynesians led policymakers to adopt policies for liberalizing all markets in the mistaken belief that "all is for the best in the best of all possible worlds provided we let well enough alone."

As we entered the twenty-first century, only the Post Keynesian school of economists remained to carry on in Keynes's analytical footsteps and develop his theory and policy prescriptions for today's real world of economic globalization.

Another Nobel Prize Winner Converts from Classical Theory to Keynes

In 1939, trying to comprehend the Keynes analysis, Sir John Hicks wrote that he "had the fortune to come upon a method of analysis.... The method of [Walrasian] General Equilibrium ... was specially designed to exhibit the economic system as a whole.... [With this method] we shall thus be able to see just why it is that Mr. Keynes reaches different results from earlier economists."[4] Hicks used this general equilibrium method to develop his famous ISLM model, which is slightly more mathematical than Samuelson's, and which he claimed explained Keynes's analytical approach. Many writers trying to get a competitive edge on the Samuelson textbook adopted this Hicksian model.

In 1971, I met John Hicks at a six-day conference on the foundations of Keynesian economics. At the conference, my participation emphasized the importance of money contracts, the existence of financial markets, and the need for liquidity. In the discussion at the end of the conference, I emphasized that a classical "general equilibrium model was not designed to, and could not answer the interesting economic questions of money, inflation and unemployment.... [I]f we [economists] insist on balancing Keynes's...economic analysis on an incompatible general equilibrium [classical theory] base we would not make any progress in macroeconomics; we would also regress to the disastrous pre-Keynesian solutions to the macro-political-economic problems."[5] By the end of the conference, Hicks informed me that the foundations of his approach to economics were closer to mine than to anyone else there. (Other participants included future Nobel Prize winners Tjalling Koopmans and Joseph Stiglitz.)

Over the next few years, Hicks and I met privately several times in the United Kingdom to continue our discussions regarding the foundation of Keynes's general theory. By the mid-1970s, Hicks was ready to admit that his model was a "potted version" of Keynes. By 1979, he was arguing that economics is embedded in calendar time and that a relationship that held in the past could not be assumed to hold in the future. In an article in the *Journal of Post Keynesian Economics* entitled "ISLM: An Explanation," Hicks denounced his mathematical model of Keynes that textbooks had adopted. Hicks wrote of this model: "As time has gone on, I have myself become dissatisfied with it" and admitted that his formulation did not describe Keynes's general theory approach at all.[6]

Finally, after reading my paper on the fallacy of rational expectations,[7] Hicks wrote to me in a letter dated February 12, 1983: "I have just been reading your RE [rational expectations] paper....I do like it very much....You have now *rationalized* my suspicions, and shown me that I missed a chance of labeling my own point of view as *nonergodic*. One needs a name like that to ram a point home."[8]

Thus Hicks, who had won a Nobel Prize for his use of general equilibrium theory, renounced his famous formulation of Keynes's framework and accepted the nonergodic view of the operation of a capitalist economy. Unfortunately, Hicks died shortly after writing this letter, and his conversion did not have any impact on the economics profession.

The 1973 Inflation: The Nail in the Coffin of Neoclassical Synthesis Keynesians

When in 1973 the OPEC cartel was able to force huge increases in the price of crude oil, inflation began to accelerate rapidly in the United States and other oil-consuming nations. The neoclassical synthesis Keynesians did not know of Keynes's writing regarding inflation and therefore did not have an immediate theoretical answer on how to resolve the problem. Instead, they considered themselves "hard scientists" and therefore looked at a statistical analysis of past economic data to explain and resolve the inflation problem of the 1970s.

Paul Samuelson and his neoclassical synthesis Keynesian colleague Robert Solow (also a Nobel Prize winner) were especially important in popularizing a historical statistical relationship where when the rate of unemployment declined, the money-wage rate and the inflation rate increased. Samuelson and Solow wrote that the historical data indicated there is an empirical trade-off for the United States where "price stability is seen to involve about 5½ percent unemployment, whereas...3 percent unemployment is seen as involving a price rise of about 4½ percent per annum."[9]

For Samuelson and Solow, the policy solution to the price inflation of the 1970s was embedded in this simple empirical analysis indicating that any increase in unemployment will always reduce the rate of inflation. They argued that the government could decide how much unemployment could be tolerated as the cost of reducing inflation. To lower inflation, all the government had to do was to use policies to increase the rate of unemployment to approximately 5.5 percent, at which point price stability would be obtained.

Unfortunately for Samuelson and Solow, the past statistical analysis was not a reliable guide to the future. Between 1973 and 1974, for example, the price level in the United States increased to 12 percent while the unemployment rate increased from 5 percent to 9 percent. Instead of following the Samuelson-Solow prediction, as unemployment rose, so did the rate of inflation. The media indicated that the United States was suffering from "stagflation"—a combination of a stagnating economy and rising unemployment. Clearly the Samuelson-Solow solution to inflation did not work, and the neoclassical synthesis Keynesian analysis fell into ill repute among economists.

At the same time, classical theorist Milton Friedman produced an argument he called the "natural rate of unemployment." He used empirical analysis to demonstrate that there was no long-run relationship between changes in the unemployment rate and changes in the rate of inflation. Thus, Friedman argued, accepting a higher rate of unemployment would not produce a lower rate of inflation. Instead, he argued that if we left it to the free market, competition would stop the inflationary forces. The neoclassical Keynesians had no response to this free market argument, even though prices continued to rise through the 1970s. The result was that "Keynesianism" was thrown in the trash basket by mainstream economists and economic advisors to politicians. Samuelson's brand of Keynesianism, which had never reflected the ideas of Keynes, was dead.

A Keynes Explanation for the 1970s Inflation Experience

Using Keynes's commodity and incomes inflation concepts and the importance of money contracts, it is easy to explain the inflation that occurred in the 1970s. When OPEC engineered an oil spike by restricting output by its members, the effect was a significant oil commodity inflation that quickly spread globally and resulted in a large increase in the cost of transporting all goods and services to market. This commodity inflation immediately increased the inflation rate as measured by the Consumer Price Index.

At that time, in the mass production industries of the United States, industrial labor unions had a cost-of-living adjustment (COLA) clause in most union contracts with employers. These COLA clauses stated that whenever the government index measuring inflation increased, an immediate equivalent percentage money-wage rate increase would be paid to all workers covered by the union contract. Consequently, as soon as the oil price commodity inflation caused the inflation rate to increase, COLA clauses set off an incomes inflation as labor costs income increases added to inflation over and above the original oil price spike. Even as unemployment rose, the COLA clauses continued to spark further inflation—a fact that was inconsistent with the Samuelson-Solow analysis, which was based on a long historical period when COLA clauses were either nonexistent or less significant. Had Samuelson and Solow understood Keynes's rejection of the ergodic axiom, they would have recognized that COLA clauses in labor contracts had changed the economic environment so that past statistical analysis was not a reliable basis for forecasting the future.

Conclusion

Paul Samuelson saved the term "Keynesian" in economic textbooks from being completely destroyed by the McCarthy anticommunist movement at the time. The cost of such a saving, however, was to sever the meaning of Keynesian theory in mainstream economic theory from its *General Theory* analytical roots. Keynes's revolution demonstrated that in a money-using, market-oriented capitalist economy, supply side market imperfections, including the fixity of money wages and/or prices or a liquidity trap, are not necessary conditions for the existence of significant and persistent unemployment. Furthermore, Keynes demonstrated that flexible wages and prices and pure competition are not sufficient conditions to ensure full employment in our economic system, even in the long run.

Samuelson's view of Keynesianism prevented Keynes's revolutionary analysis from sweeping mainstream economics off its classical theory axiomatic foundations. Neoclassical synthesis Keynesianism coming at the same time as mathematics in economics became popular provided a double whammy that aborted Keynes's revolutionary theory. What passed as conventional economic wisdom of mainstream economists at the beginning of the twenty-first century is nothing more than high-tech and more mathematical versions of nineteenth-century classical Walrasian general equilibrium theory.

In winning the battle against the forces trying to prevent the teaching of suspected communist-inspired Keynesian economics in our universities, Samuelson ultimately lost the war that Keynes had launched to eliminate the classical theoretical analysis as the basis for real-world economic problems of employment, interest, and money. In 1986, Lorie Tarshis recognized this fact when he noted: "I never felt that Keynes was being followed with full adherence or full understanding of what he had written. I still feel that way."[10]

Today mainstream economics—whether it goes under the title of old neoclassical Keynesians, New Keynesians, old classical or new classical theorists, Arrow-Debreu-Walrasian economics, post-Walrasian theory, behavioral economic theory—still relies on the classical axioms that Keynes discarded in his attempt to make economics relevant to the real-world problems of unemployment and international trade and international payments. As a result, these problems still plague much of the real world in the globalized economy of the twenty-first century.

I hope that this book will encourage economists and political economic advisors to reexamine Keynes's ideas; they remain the greatest hope for producing a prosperous, civilized capitalist economy.

NOTES

Chapter 1

1. J. M. Keynes, *The General Theory of Employment, Interest and Money* (London: Macmillan, 1936), 380.
2. I. Adelman, "Long Term Economic Development," Working Paper No. 589, California Agricultural Experiment Station, Berkeley, March 1991, p. 2.

Chapter 2

1. Note I use the term "leveraging," a nice code word that has become popular in recent years, rather than saying "going into debt."
2. These leveraged investors of 1929 were, in some sense, the equivalent of the hedge funds of recent years, where the latter take on heavily leveraged positions in financial markets around the world.
3. By comparison, we might note that during the first years of the twenty-first century, unregulated hedge funds, those mysterious investment vehicles that only the rich can invest in, often leveraged their position in financial assets by as much as, or more than, a 19-to-1 ratio. One of the reasons often given for the collapse of prices in financial markets in 2008 was that many hedge funds found it difficult to meet the debt obligations used to finance their portfolio holdings. This hedge fund problem resembles what the small investors who bought on margin faced in 1929 when stock prices started a precipitous decline.

4. H. Hoover, *The Memoir of Herbert Hoover: The Great Depression, 1929–1941* (New York: Macmillan, 1952), 257.

5. D. Moggridge, ed., *The Collected Writings of John Maynard Keynes*, vol. 13 (London: Macmillan, 1973), 492–93.

6. J. M. Keynes, *A Tract on Monetary Reform* (1923), reprinted as *The Collected Writings of John Maynard Keynes*, vol. 4 (London: Macmillan, 1971).

7. Unfortunately, in the 1930s, the official unemployment rate counted as unemployed those workers employed by the government in Works Projects Administration and other government programs. Only workers who had jobs in the private sector were counted as employed. Thus, the unofficial unemployment rate tries to ensure that people who had full-time jobs in Roosevelt's "workfare" programs are not counted as unemployed.

8. J. M. Keynes, *The General Theory of Employment, Interest and Money* (London: Macmillan, 1936), 9.

Chapter 3

1. L. H. Summers and V. P. Summers, "When Financial Markets Work Too Well: A Cautious Case for a Securities Transactions Tax," *Journal of Financial Services* 3 (1989): 166.

2. R. E. Lucas, "Tobin and Monetarism: A Review Article," *Journal of Economic Literature* 19 (1981): 563.

Chapter 4

1. J. M. Keynes, *The General Theory of Employment, Interest and Money* (London: Macmillan, 1936), 16.

2. R. Skidelsky, *John Maynard Keynes: The Economist as Saviour, 1920–1937* (London: Macmillan, 1992), 223.

3. Classical theorists avoid recognizing this depressing effect of savings behavior by assuming that whenever any individual saves a dollar out of income, there is another buyer who simultaneously is borrowing that dollar in order to dissave (i.e., to spend a dollar more than that buyer's income).

Chapter 5

1. O. Blanchard, "Why Does Money Affect Output?" in *Handbook of Monetary Economics*, vol. 2, ed. B. M. Friedman and F. H. Hahn (New York: North Holland, 1990), 828.
2. J. M. Keynes, "A Monetary Theory of Production" (1933), reprinted in *The Collected Writings of John Maynard Keynes*, vol. 13, ed. D. Moggridge (London: Macmillan, 1973), 408–9.
3. J. K. Galbraith, "On Post Keynesian Economics," *Journal of Post Keynesian Economics* 1 (1978): 8–9.
4. H. Hoover, *The Memoirs of Herbert Hoover: The Great Depression, 1929–1941* (New York: Macmillan, 1952), 30.

Chapter 6

1. An earlier version of the argument that follows was published in *Challenge* 51, no. 3 (May–June 2008): 43–56. Copyright 2008 by M. E. Shape, Inc. Reprinted with permission. All rights reserved. Not for reproduction.
2. If the classical efficient market theory is buttressed by the assumption of rational expectations, then expectations about the long run ensure that short-run market prices do not get far out of line with their long-run fundamentals-determined price.
3. *Wall Street Journal*, October 18, 2001, A1.
4. *Repos*, short for *repurchase agreements*, are contracts for the sale and future repurchase of a financial asset, most often Treasury securities. On the termination date, the seller repurchases the asset at the same price at which he or she sold it, and pays interest for the use of the funds. Although legally a sequential pair of sales, in effect *a repo is a short-term interest-bearing loan against collateral*.
5. I emphasized the need for a revived Resolution Trust Corporation to help solve the financial market crisis that was initiated with the subprime mortgage problem in my paper "How to Solve the U.S. Housing Mess and Avoid a Recession: A Revised HOLC and RTC," Policy Note, Schwartz Center for Economic Policy Analysis, The New School, January 2008.

6. Before the day's auction begins, investment bankers typically provide "price talk" to their clients indicating a range of likely clearing rates for that auction. This range is based on a number of factors, including the issuer's credit rating, the last clearance rate for this and similar issues, and general macroeconomic conditions.

7. J. Anderson and V. Bajaj, "New Trouble in Auction Rate Securities," *New York Times*, February 15, 2008, D4.

Chapter 7

1. J. M. Keynes, "National Self-Sufficiency" (1933), reprinted in *The Collected Writings of John Maynard Keynes*, vol. 21, ed. D. Moggridge (London: Macmillan, 1982), 238.

2. This assumes that transportation costs do not completely offset the lower labor costs per unit.

Chapter 8

1. J. M. Keynes, *Post-War Currency Policy* (1941), reprinted in *The Collected Writings of John Maynard Keynes*, vol. 25, ed. D. Moggridge (London: Macmillan, 1980), 27.

2. Ibid., 21–22.

3. P. Davidson, *Post Keynesian Macroeconomic Theory: A Foundation for Succesful Economic Policies in the 21st Century* (Cheltenham, UK: Elgar, 1994).

Chapter 9

1. J. M. Keynes, *The General Theory of Employment, Interest and Money* (London: Macmillan, 1936), 378.

2. Ibid., 131.

3. S. P. Dunn, *The Uncertain Foundations of Post Keynesian Economics* (London: Routledge, 2008), 187.

Chapter 10

1. R. Skidelsky, *John Maynard Keynes: Hopes Betrayed, 1883–1920* (London: Macmillan, 1983), 175.
2. R. F. Harrod, *The Life of John Maynard Keynes* (London: Macmillan, 1951), 203.
3. Skidelsky, *John Maynard Keynes: Hopes Betrayed*, 374–75.
4. Ibid., 384.

Appendix

1. R. Skidelsky, *John Maynard Keynes: The Economist as Saviour, 1920–1937* (London: Macmillan, 1992), 512.
2. N. G. Mankiw, "The Reincarnation of Keynesian Economics," *European Economic Record* 36 (1992): 561.
3. D. Colander and H. Landreth, *The Coming of Keynesianism to America* (Cheltenham, UK: Elgar, 1996), 159–60.
4. J. R. Hicks, *Value and Capital*, 2nd ed. (Oxford: Oxford University Press, 1946), 1–4.
5. See Davidson's discussion in *The Microfoundations of Macroeconomics*, ed. G. C. Harcourt. Unfortunately, my prediction involving the progress in macroeconomics has come true.
6. J. R. Hicks, "ISLM: An Explanation," *Journal of Post Keynesian Economics* 3 (1980–81): 139.
7. P. Davidson, "Rational Expectations: A Fallacious Foundation for Studying Crucial Decision-Making Processes," *Journal of Post Keynesian Economics* 5 (1982–83): 182–97.
8. This letter is available in the collection of my correspondence that is on deposit at the Duke University Library Archives of economists' correspondence and writings.
9. P. A. Samuelson and R. M. Solow, "Analytical Aspects of Anti-Inflation Policy," *American Economic Review Papers and Proceedings* 50 (1960): 192–93.
10. Colander and Landreth, *The Coming of Keynesianism to America*, 72.

BIBLIOGRAPHY

Adelman, I. "Long Term Economic Development," Working Paper No. 589, California Agricultural Experiment Station, Berkeley (March 1991).

Anderson, J., and Bajaj, V. "New Trouble in Auction Rate Securities," *New York Times*, February 15, 2008.

Arrow, K. J., and Hahn, F. H. *General Competitive Equilibrium*. San Francisco: Holden-Day, 1971.

Berle, A. A., and Means, G. C. *The Modern Corporation and Private Property*. New York: Commerce Clearing House, 1932.

Bernstein, P. L. *Against the Gods*. New York: John Wiley & Sons, 1996.

Blanchard, O. "Why Does Money Affect Output?" in *Handbook of Monetary Economics*, vol. 2, ed. B. M. Friedman and F. H. Hahn. New York: North Holland, 1990.

Buckley, W. F. *God and Man at Yale*. Chicago: Henry Regnery, 1951.

Colander, D. C., and Landreth, H. *The Coming of Keynesianism to America*. Cheltenham, UK: Elgar, 1996.

Davidson, P. "Discussion of the Paper by Professor Leijonhufvud," in *The Microfoundations of Macroeconomics*, ed. G. C. Harcourt. London: Macmillan, 1977.

Davidson, P. "Rational Expectations: A Fallacious Foundation for Studying Crucial Decision-Making Processes," *Journal of Post Keynesian Economics* 5 (1982–83).

Davidson, P. *Post Keynesian Macroeconomic Theory*. Cheltenham, UK: Elgar, 1994.

Davidson, P. *Financial Markets, Money and the Real World*. Cheltenham, UK: Elgar, 2002.

Davidson, P. "How to Solve the U.S. Housing Problem and Avoid Recession: A Revived HOLC and RTC," Policy Note, Schwartz Center for Economic Policy Analysis (January 2008).

Davidson, P. "Securitization, Liquidity and Market Failure," *Challenge* 51, no. 3 (May–June 2008).

Dunn, S. P. *The Uncertain Foundations of Post Keynesian Economics.* London: Routledge, 2008.

Friedman, M. "Comments on the Critics," in *Milton Friedman's Monetary Framework: A Debate with His Critics*, ed. R. J. Gordon. Chicago: University of Chicago Press, 1974.

Friedman, M. "Markets to the Rescue," *Wall Street Journal*, October 12, 1998.

Galbraith, J. K. *The Affluent Society.* New York: Houghton Mifflin, 1957.

Galbraith, J. K. "On Post Keynesian Economics," *Journal of Post Keynesian Economics* 1 (1978).

Harrod, R. F. *The Life of John Maynard Keynes.* London: Macmillan, 1951.

Hicks, J. R. "Mr. Keynes and the Classics: A Suggested Interpretation," *Econometrica* 5 (1937).

Hicks, J. R. *Value and Capital*, 2nd ed. Oxford: Oxford University Press, 1946.

Hicks, J. R. "Some Questions of Time in Economics," in *Evolution, Welfare and Time in Economics*, ed. A. M. Tang et al. Lexington, MA: Heath Books, 1976.

Hicks, J. R. *Causality in Economics.* New York: Basic Books, 1979.

Hicks, J. R. "ISLM: An Explanation," *Journal of Post Keynesian Economics* 3 (1980–81).

Hoover, H. *The Memoirs of Herbert Hoover: The Great Depression, 1929–1941.* New York: Macmillan, 1952.

Keynes, J. M. (1919). *The Economic Consequences of the Peace.* Reprinted as *The Collected Writings of John Maynard Keynes*, vol. 2, ed. D. Moggridge. London: Macmillan, 1971.

Keynes, J. M. (1923). *A Tract on Monetary Reform.* Reprinted as *The Collected Writings of John Maynard Keynes*, vol. 4, ed. D. Moggridge. London: Macmillan, 1971.

Keynes, J. M. (1930). *A Treatise on Money.* Reprinted as *The Collected Writings of John Maynard Keynes*, vols. 5 and 6, ed. D. Moggridge. London: Macmillan, 1971.

Keynes, J. M. (1933). "National Self-Sufficiency." Reprinted in *The Collected Writings of John Maynard Keynes*, vol. 21, ed. D. Moggridge. London: Macmillan, 1982.

Keynes, J. M. (1935). January 1, 1935, letter to George Bernard Shaw. Reprinted in *The Collected Writings of John Maynard Keynes*, vol. 13, ed. D. Moggridge. London: Macmillan, 1971.

Keynes, J. M. (1935). "A Monetary Theory of Production." Reprinted in *The Collected Writings of John Maynard Keynes*, vol. 13, ed. D. Moggridge. London: Macmillan, 1973.

Keynes, J. M. (1936). *The General Theory of Employment, Interest and Money*, German language ed. Berlin: Dunker and Humboldt.

Keynes, J. M. (1936). *The General Theory of Employment, Interest and Money.* Reprinted in *The Collected Writings of John Maynard Keynes*, vol. 7, ed. D. Moggridge. London: Macmillan, 1973.

Keynes, J. M. (1941). "Post-War Currency Policy." Reprinted in *The Collected Writings of John Maynard Keynes*, vol. 25, ed. D. Moggridge. London: Macmillan, 1980.

Lucas, R. E. "Understanding Business Cycles," in *Stabilization of the Domestic and International Economy*, ed. K. Brunner and A. H. Meltzer, *Carnegie Mellon Conference on Public Policy* 5 (1977).

Lucas, R. E. "Tobin and Monetarism: A Review Article," *Journal of Economic Literature* 19 (1981).

Lucas, R. E., and Sargent, T. J. *Rational Expectations of Econometric Practices*. Minneapolis: University of Minnesota Press, 1981.

Mankiw, N. G. "The Reincarnation of Keynesian Economics," *European Economic Record* 36 (1992).

Moore, G. E. *Principia Ethica*. Cambridge: Cambridge University Press, 1903.

Ricardo, D. *On the Principles of Political Economy and Taxation*. London: Macmillan, 1817.

Samuelson, P. A. *Economics: An Introductory Analysis*. New York: McGraw-Hill, 1948.

Samuelson, P. A. *Foundations of Economic Analysis*. Cambridge, MA: Harvard University Press, 1947.

Samuelson, P. A. "Classical and Neoclassical Theory," in *Monetary Theory*, ed. R. W. Clower. London: Penguin, 1969.

Samuelson, P. A., and Solow, R. M. "Analytical Aspects of Anti-Inflation Policy," *American Economic Review Papers and Proceedings* 50 (1960).

Skidelsky, R. *John Maynard Keynes: Economist, Philosopher, Statesman, 1883–1946*. London: Macmillan, 2003.

Skidelsky, R. *John Maynard Keynes: The Economist as Saviour, 1920–1937*. London: Macmillan, 1992.

Skidelsky, R. *John Maynard Keynes Fighting for Britain*. London: Macmillan, 2000.

Skidelsky, R. *John Maynard Keynes: Hopes Betrayed, 1883–1920*. London: Macmillan, 1983.

Skidelsky, R. *Keynes*. Oxford: Oxford University Press, 1996.

Smith, A. (1776). *An Inquiry into the Wealth of Nations*. Reprinted as *An Inquiry into the Wealth of Nations*. New York: Modern Library, 1937.

Summers, L. H., and Summers, V. P. "When Financial Markets Work Too Well: A Cautious Case for a Securities Transactions Tax," *Journal of Financial Services* 3 (1989).

Uchitelle, L. *The Disposable American: Layoffs and Their Consequences*. New York: Knopf, 2006.

Walras, L. (1874). *Elements of Pure Economics*. London: Allen and Unwin, 1954.

Weintraub, S. "An Incomes Policy to Stop Inflation," *Lloyds Bank Review* (1971).

INDEX